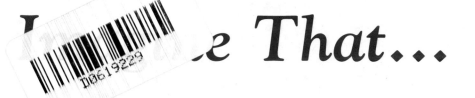

Imagine That...

A Handbook of Creative
Learning Activities for the Classroom

Stephen Bowkett

Published by Network Educational Press Ltd.
PO Box 635
Stafford
ST16 1BF

First Published 1997
First Reprint 2001
© Stephen Bowkett 1997

ISBN 1 85539 043 4

Edited by Carol Thompson
and Chris Griffin
Design/Graphics and Layout by
Neil Hawkins of Devine Design

Printed in Great Britain by
MPG Books Ltd., Bodmin, Cornwall.

CONTENTS

> **Teachers open the door,
> but you must enter
> by yourself.**

Chinese proverb

Introduction

"The mind is not a vessel to be filled but a fire to be lighted."

(Plutarch)

1. What's this?

2. If you could say ten words to save the world from destruction, what would they be?

3. Describe the smell of petrol (not whether you like the smell or not).

4. What are you going to do tonight?

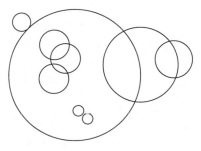

5. Find a link between these words.

   CRYSTAL   JOINT   SET   FAR   HANDLE

6. When were you last envious? What did it feel like exactly?

7. It's 4.30 p.m. on December 21st, a clear, frosty evening. What do you see, hear, feel?

8. How could you use this as a teaching device?

9. If you could become younger and more physically attractive at the expense of someone else's youth and beauty, would you do so? What if this person was very close to you, would that affect your decision? If you answered *yes* to the first question, justify yourself.

10. What are the wisest words you've ever heard?

11. What are the stupidest words you've ever heard?

12. What do you think 'being creative' involves?

Hopefully, you will agree that questions such as these allow teachers to realise that:

- opinions count as valued and valid information
- some questions have answers which are neither 'good' nor 'bad', but more, or less, useful
- part of the process of creative learning is to 'go inside' yourself and think about what you already know, in relation to new information and ideas being offered.

Imagine That... offers a diverse range of activities based on these principles, helping students to realise their full imaginative potential.

The Ping Process

My attitude towards becoming more creative can be summed up as follows:

- Everything is material for creative thinking.
- There are no right answers; there are only answers which are more, or less, useful.
- You need to have lots of ideas to have some good ideas.
- Never be satisfied with the first answer or solution.
- There is no automatic link between age, wisdom, authority and originality.
- Look children, hailstones. Let's rush out!
- Intellectual achievement is not the same as creativity.
- 'Reactive' thinking (guess the answer) is not of itself creative.
- We all have imaginations. We all have the capacity to improve them.
- Failure is not falling down, but staying down.
- The creative thinker is an opportunist.
- Content is pointless without process.
- Subject areas should ideally be processes of thinking, feeling, doing.
- Expectations determine outcomes.
- There are three golden rules to becoming a more creative thinker: practise, practise, practise!

Using This Book

I have arranged the book into a number of broad sections. Each section contains activities which you can use on a stand alone basis. Some activities take just a few minutes, providing stimulus games or warm up sessions. Others are more elaborate: they need preparation and could last for a number of lessons or time slots.

The main value of the activities, however, is in using them in combination and in a wide range of subject areas. This will help you to develop your pupils' creative thinking across the curriculum.

The activities link strongly with English. For example, the Programme of Study for Speaking and Listening at Key Stage 2 English requires that:

Pupils should be given opportunities to talk for a range of purposes, including:

> exploring, developing and explaining ideas;
> planning, predicting and investigating;
> sharing ideas, insights and opinions;
> reading aloud, telling and enacting stories and poems;
> reporting and describing events and observations;
> presenting to audiences, live or on tape.

The National Curriculum *(1995 DfEE Crown Copyright)*

This book provides pupils with a wide range of opportunities to develop these skills in genuine contexts. It is also compatible with the Speaking and Listening Programmes of Study at Key Stages 3 and 4, and provides opportunities for different modes of writing. The activities also have very clear links with Drama and Personal and Social Education.

In addition, the activities are relevant to the National Curriculum requirements of other subjects. They can develop the use and application of Mathematics; help learners to investigate scientific knowledge; and help them discover the characteristics of materials in Design and Technology. The activities can develop pupils' awareness of chronology and change in History; provide motivating techniques to investigate places and themes in Geography; and enhance visual literacy in Art.

The Activities/National Curriculum matrix (p.10) provides examples of how the activities can be used when teaching the National Curriculum. These examples are not exhaustive. The activities can be applied to other National Curriculum teaching and learning aims.

Examples of how to use the activities to teach National Curriculum Topics

	English	Maths.	Science	History		Geography	Design Technology	Art
	Develop Ability to Write Narrative	Visualise and Describe Shapes & Movement	Blood Circulation	Work & Leisure in a Tudor Town	Overview of World War 1	Issue in a Settlement *(e.g. environmental)*	Consider Appearance, Function, Safety & Reliability	Compare Ideas, Methods & Approaches
	KS3/4	**KS2**	**KS2**	**KS2**	**KS3**	**KS2**	**KS2**	**KS2**
Journey though My Body (p.123)			✓					
I am a Ship (p.114)		✓	✓			✓		
Board Games (p.123)			✓			✓		
Theme Cards (p.17)	✓		✓		✓	✓		✓
Footprints (p.66)							✓	
Heath Robinson (p.77)		✓					✓	
How to Prevent (p.95)							✓	
The Why Game (p.102)						✓	✓	
Circles (p.47)	✓			✓	✓			
Ten Questions (p.53)	✓			✓	✓			
Magazine Editor (p.109)				✓		✓		
Word Chain (p.27)					✓	✓		
Picture Sequences (p.32)	✓					✓		✓
Odd One Out (p.30)					✓			
What If? (p.86)					✓			
Parallel World (p.92)	✓				✓	✓		
Habitat (p.73)				✓		✓		
Now Collage (p.121)				✓		✓		✓
Constellations (p.28)								✓
Colour Spiders								✓
Abstract Art (p.43)		✓						✓
Symbols (p.45)		✓						✓
One Unique Detail (p.70)	✓							✓
Brainstorming (p.21)	✓							
Inscape (p.68)	✓							✓
Context Sentences (p.90)	✓							
Dice Journey (p.177)	✓							
Sensory Stimulus (p.58)		✓						
Freeze Frame		✓			✓			
Peas in a Pod (p.142)		✓						
A Day in the Life				✓				

Of course, teachers will develop their own repertoire of favourite techniques to use with their learners and apply these across the curriculum. For example, a dice journey can be used to explore a medieval village, trace the life cycle of flowering plants, track the course of a river from source to estuary, and create a narrative story.

What teachers will especially value is the degree of pupil engagement which the activities generate. This leads to the pupils remaining on task, and, as we all know, when pupils are on task, the quality of their learning is enhanced.

The following will help you to make the most of the book:

Equipment and Techniques

The introduction contains a section outlining some of the equipment you will need and some of the basic teaching and classroom organisation techniques which underpin the book. Do not be put off by the word equipment. I am not talking about expensive hi-tech machinery, but simple items that can be made from everyday materials.

The Sections

I have divided the book into sections, each one containing activities which relate to the overall theme of the section. I have also provided an introduction for each section, which considers the benefits and potential uses of the activities.

The Activities

Each activity consists of a basic/core activity plus suggestions for extension and variation. Links with other activities in the book are also listed.

Practicalities Box

Each activity has a *Practicalities Box* which provides at-a-glance information about organising the activity: grouping the students; how much time you will need; equipment required; and any other important points you need to know before you begin. As a teacher of some 20 years experience I am very conscious of the need to address the nuts and bolts of any new method. Just like the pupils I always want to know what I have to do.

The *Practicalities Box* refers solely to the basic activity. Extension and variations may require extra equipment and time.

I have included further notes and tips where necessary.

Sequence of Activities

You can do the activities in any order. You will find that by using the book regularly, perhaps focusing on those activities you like or which you feel are most effective, the techniques will become second nature and the ability to think creatively will develop rapidly.

Activities for Teachers

At the back of the book you will find a section aimed at teachers. The section gives them a chance to develop their own creative thinking skills through a series of tasks and activities which I have used with success on in-service training courses.

A Model Of The Mind

I believe that ideas happen because we want them to. My experience is also that the appearance of an idea (that lovely moment in comic strips when the lightbulb turns on in a thought-bubble) is accompanied by a wonderful sense of excitement, a feeling of promise and pleasurable anticipation. In short, an idea seems to come from some place other than the intellectual conscious part of the mind; and it is accompanied by powerful emotions that have a lot to do with the motivation required to see that idea through to completion.

I spent many years relying on the Muse before I came across a simple, effective and verifiable model of the mind that accounted for all the characteristics of what I call the Ping Process – wanting ideas, having lots of them, and turning the most useful ones into finished projects: stories, poems, pieces of non-fiction, or the best way to use up the scraps of food left in the fridge. Any model of the mind is probably simplistic (such as the recent fashion in left brain/ right brain thinking). But that doesn't matter, because I'm interested in manipulating the picture on the screen, not in how the TV is wired up to produce the image in the first place.

The conscious part of the mind is the part that's alert, awake and aware on a moment-by-moment basis. The point of conscious attention is usually focused externally, though if the outside world is not stimulating us, we begin to daydream; that is, we internalise our attention and fantasise.

We are alert to the world because we have to be. We receive impressions through our senses, 'process the data' by using our intellectual abilities and/or following hunches, and make decisions about what and what not to do for the best.

Part of our awareness is also an awareness of self – or that part of our self which impinges upon our consciousness: our appearance, our immediate mood, our immediate plans... This involvement with the 'surface self' sparks memories for comparison with the here-and-now, and allows for imaginative anticipation of the future; of thinking what might be the consequences of present actions.

In other words, the conscious mind, like the captain of the ship, makes decisions which will hopefully allow us to steer a safe, happy and healthy course through life.

What I call 'the subconscious' is merely a convenient label for all the processes that occur largely beyond the realm of conscious awareness and control.

Stated most simply, the subconscious part of the mind – the crew of the ship – has two basic functions. Firstly, the subconscious is in ultimate and fundamental control of the body. Hundreds of thousands of things happen inside each of us every moment of every minute all through our lives, without our having to consciously monitor or control them. And yet our body does not 'run itself': it is not a machine without a guidance system. For convenience, I say that the control and guidance of the body occurs at the subconscious level.

The other principal function of the subconscious is to create a 'map of reality' – a blueprint of what we think the world is like beyond our skins. This it does through a continual process of associating incoming information with that which has been laid down in the past. This blueprint is necessarily subjective, because it is based on our own unique life experiences, plus information generated and processed by the conscious part of the mind, then fed back to the subconscious.

There are several ideas implicit in the above:
- The body and mind are intimately connected, so that it's pointless to talk about one without reference to the other.
- Thoughts, feelings and behaviours form an unbroken loop within every individual. By *thoughts*, I mean conscious decisions and ideas, and subconscious mental processes. By *feelings*, I mean our conscious day-to-day moods and our underlying outlook on life. By *behaviours*, I mean our conscious voluntary actions, and the state of our bodies under the guidance and control of the subconscious part of the mind.
- The fruits of the imagination (the capacity to manipulate our own thoughts) lie in the conscious mind, while the roots go deep into the subconscious.
- The conscious mind decides, and the subconscious mind allows to happen, or brings to fruition. This principle has profound implications for one's well-being and for the 'mechanism' of creative thinking – the Ping Process.

For me, creative thinking boils down to ways of opening up the channels of communication between the conscious and subconscious parts of the mind, in line with the principles outlined above. The Ping Process involves a large and vital emotional component – creative thinking necessarily needs to be fun. Once that link is established, creativity and enjoyment will feed each other beneficially, leading in the end to the more valuable emotional rewards of increased confidence and self-esteem, satisfaction, pride-in-achievement, and a deep sense of fulfilment based on individual endeavour.

The point also needs to be made that the content of any subject or area of knowledge is of little use unless it is fuel to feed the fire of creative thought. That creative thought, in an ideal world, would be independent and energetic, the property of the individual: it would be judged by the individual herself, partly on its 'fun factor', but more lastingly on its usefulness in furthering the understanding of the thinker. It would not be manipulated or otherwise controlled by outside 'authorities' unless such input respected the principles of the Ping Process and the uniqueness of the individual.

The fact that such an idea smacks of a liberalism quite out of tune with the current machinery of the educational system in this country does not detract from the effectiveness of developing creative thinking towards conventional outcomes; i.e., helping students to get better marks in tests. I assert that children will do their best (in all senses of the word) if the facts they are fed mean something to them personally, and if the process of meaning-making is an enjoyable one. Those aims are not beyond the scope or abilities of any teacher or parent reading this book, and it is my sincere hope that the activities in *Imagine That...* go some way towards achieving them.

A Model of the Mind

The Outside World

The Conscious Self

The Decision Maker -
intellectual abilities / reasoning / logic / common sense
'ego' / will power
the here-and-now active and alive
the fruits of creative thinking

The Inside World

The Subconscious Self

The 'Automatic Pilot' -
body monitoring, guidance & control /
map of reality – beliefs, values, emotional landscape
the past active and alive
the roots of creative thinking

INSTRESS	**INSCAPE**
the force expressing uniqueness	**the inner landscape**
	individual uniqueness

Basic Equipment

Notebooks

Although ideas can come vividly and powerfully into the head, they are also fleeting and easily forgotten if they're not written down at once. Notebooks, of course, form part of the standard kit of any student, and for the creative thinker they are absolutely essential. Many teachers across the subject range establish the regime of a book for rough notes and early drafts, and a 'best book' for the finished product. I would like to suggest also the provision of an 'ideas and impressions' book to complement the system that's already used.

With ongoing practice of the techniques and activities in *Imagine That...*, students will increasingly be coming up with ideas. The 'I & I' book will form a repository of this raw material, plus a place where the creative thinker can begin to develop the structure of particular ideas that look likely to bear the best fruit. Ideas books might be subject-specific, but greater opportunities will be allowed for creative thinking if students are encouraged to jot down all of their ideas in the *same* book. It's likely that by doing this, useful cross-connections will be made between subjects; these links carry greater significance and meaning for the individual student who has made them.

What's important is establishing the *habit* of recording ideas as they come. Quite without struggling for it, students will soon find that they have accumulated far more ideas than they can ever develop into finished products.

Decision Dice

On the day-to-day level of making decisions, choosing options, or working effectively through many of the activities in this book, so-called *decision dice* form a handy low-tech accoutrement to the creative process.

The specific use of dice is explained in the activities themselves. For the purposes of assembling equipment for *Imagine That...*, it is enough to know now that a bag of about twenty dice will be needed. I also employ the fancy polyhedral dice you can buy at places like Games Workshop; and I have a big sponge dice which I use when I do role-play work, or take creative thinking off the page and into the gym, hall or playing field.

As you will see in techniques like *Dice Journey* (p.177), dice form a simple but effective mechanism for making group dynamics more effective and for creating flexibility within a structure.

Spinner

Spinners have been used by children for generations to see 'who goes next', and can be employed for the same purpose in creative thinking.

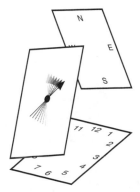

The spinner I carry as part of my kit is years old and comes with a set of notes written by Ray Bull, Associate Editor of the old Nuffield 5-11 Maths Project. The accompanying spinner cards can be used for counting exercises, demonstrating simple rules of arithmetic, for tallying, fraction recognition and so on...

Card Banks

Card banks are cheap, reliable, flexible and, once they are established, easy to maintain and develop. Another plus is that card banks can be made to order, and at quite short notice, to suit a particular theme, topic or series of lessons. Creating card banks can even be a class or group exercise in itself: if you are doing, say, onomatopoeia (sound words) with one group, have another group write *hiss, bang, splash*, and fifty other onomatopoeic words on 127x76mm file cards. Many other types of *word banks* can be compiled in this way. This not only encourages dictionary and thesaurus use and an attentiveness to spelling, but also fixes the concept more firmly in the minds of the students making the cards. Subsequently the onomatopoeia card bank can be used for all kinds of language-related topics, and across the subject range in a great variety of ways.

Before moving on, try to think of ten ways, in as many different subjects as possible, of using the onomatopoeia card bank...

Now think of another twenty themes for card banks...

And of course you're not limited to single words on cards. Other kinds of banks include:-
- pictures from magazines, newspapers, etc. (see below)
- abstract art, both professional and 'home made'
- words and ideas linked by theme, sound, genre, and so on
- names of people, places, objects...
- short descriptions of people, places, objects, emotions, situations...
- opening / closing lines or paragraphs from stories

And how many others?

Picture Banks

Collections of visual material can form a cheap and flexible resource in any classroom. Such a resource is easily assembled – again, students can help create picture banks as they did the card banks. And if the pictures are mounted on card and sleeved in plastic, the result looks colourful, professional and can last for years.

Such picture banks, like card banks generally, have a wide application for creative thinking in all areas of the curriculum. More fundamentally, it's difficult to come up with ideas, let alone good ones, out of thin air. Since most of the information we absorb about the world is visual, it makes sense to boost and accelerate the learning process by employing visuals whenever possible to support the information content of lessons. Pictures (and posters, video, CD-ROM, etc.) add colour, variety and interest even to the most abstract, obtuse and text-based lessons.

Think of ten varieties of picture banks – and ten curriculum areas where they could be used. Further ideas and links can be found in the activities that follow.

Sundries Bag

Also known to the great delight and amusement of students as a 'feely-bag'! This is basically a 3D version of a *Picture Bank* (see p.16); simply a collection of interesting objects displaying a variety of shapes, sizes, textures and other qualities.

The most basic use of the sundries bag is to have students describe the objects, without naming them, either by feeling them while they are inside the bag (the objects, not the students), or by looking at them closely and describing them to other students who cannot see the objects. This sharpens up one's powers of observation and gives good practice in language use.

Other activities include giving small groups a number of sundry objects at random and asking them to link the objects in some way – perhaps through a storyline or piece of drama. An extension of this idea is to give out selections of objects and ask for them to be linked within a theme.

Pairs of objects can be compared and contrasted. Objects can be placed in order of familiarity, complexity of manufacture or production, or by the significance they have for individual students. They can also form the basis of a 'this reminds me' game, and be linked to free association work, guided or scripted fantasies...

And aside from a good deal of vocabulary work (what exactly is the difference between *knobbly* and *rough*?), discussion of the objects can be opened out to explore values, aesthetics, problem-solving skills (100 things to do with a paperclip, etc.), and many other topics.

As with most of the activities which follow, the effectiveness and diversity-of-use of the *Sundries Bag* depends entirely upon the imaginations of the users.

Theme Cards

The composition of theme cards forms a useful and creative activity in itself; but the cards can then be used as a resource bank to feed further thinking and the development of ideas in conjunction with other *Imagine That...* tools.

Time flies

A typical card consists of a collection of images and pieces of information linked by a theme. For instance, a picture might be combined with an abstract design or some symbols, a quotation or motto, some scientific facts and figures, a fragment of conversation or an opinion, a piece of musical notation, and so on. Cards can be created for all ages and abilities, and targeted towards particular subjects and areas of the curriculum: they can be very broadly based (the Environment) or finely focused (a specific story or poem). Use the cards

'But on the shores of Time each leaves some trace of its passage...'

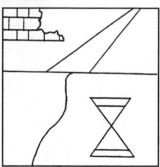

as a starting point for discussion, story making, art, drama, scientific investigation, review and revision of work topics, consolidating abstract or difficult ideas, etc.

Badgemaker

One of the guiding principles of the activities in this book is that they should be cheap and low-tech (i.e., less to go wrong). But if you do happen to have a badgemaker in the school, you can use badges in interesting ways:

- Have badges with individual words printed on them. In an open space, ask children (wearing the badges) to mingle until they come up with interesting word combinations that suggest a theme, story, character, etc.
- Make colour / texture / word badges and run the activity above.
- Make picture badges that suggest or tell a story. Groups try to line up in the right (i.e.. narrative) order.
- Make badges with cartoon characters on them and have groups role-play those characters, make up stories about them, find a motto that suits them, etc.
- Use badges and coloured dots or stickers to allow children to accumulate rewards through the week.

Basic Techniques

Picture Discussion

This is one of the simplest *Imagine That...* activities, but also one of the most versatile and powerful in developing discussion and socialisation skills, powers of observation and deduction, and boosting self-confidence in having valid and valued ideas.

Basic activity

Pick a picture from the *Picture Bank* (see p.16) and invite students to comment on it. Explain that even the most obvious points are acceptable – and establish early the ethos that everyone's observations are equally important. What's likely to happen is that, indeed, students will notice the picture's most prominent features first: let the run of ideas take its course before directing the students' attention towards more particular and/or subtle features of the picture, or asking the group to extrapolate from what is visible.

Ways of opening-out the activity include:
- Encourage deduction based on what the group can see. For example, 'The trees have no leaves, so it's likely to be late autumn or winter'; 'There are three policemen across the road, so maybe there's been some trouble..'; 'By the expression on that person's face, I think she's just had a quarrel'.
- Have students discuss what may lie beyond the frame of the picture.
- Ask students to step into the picture imaginatively and take a look around.
- Focus on the different sensory modalities – what colours are apparent in the picture (do this even if the visual is black-and-white!); what sounds might you expect to hear in the picture; what smells; what textures? Encourage the easy flow of language and maintain the group's enthusiasm for the activity through your own.
- Use time distortion techniques. Imagine you can speed up time – what changes in the picture, and how; what stays the same? Freeze time and now take a look at otherwise rapidly moving objects. Step back an hour and discuss what's happened up to the point when the photograph was taken. Or move time on and ask what might happen now.
- Change the observer's point-of-view. Add or subtract features of the scene and see what happens.

And so on. The game can become powerfully absorbing and highly entertaining, allowing children to express themselves creatively within a comfortable context, free from the concern of saying the right thing (or feeling foolish through saying the wrong thing!).

The activity has no time limit; it runs just as long as people are interested. There need be no predetermined aims; the game can be used as a filler in a spare ten minutes – although *Picture Discussion* can also form part of a highly structured sequence of activities with many planned and hoped-for outcomes.

Frequently, discussion overspills into more general themes and the students' own personal experiences. This process of easy reflection or reminiscence remains a basic stimulus to creative thinking and a key tool for establishing that flexibility within a user-friendly structure. It can, of course, also be utilised and directed into other areas and contexts, such as allowing learners to weave their own experiences into story-making activities ('write about what you know' being an often quoted golden rule); giving them practice in accessing memories through a variety of sensory modalities – visual, auditory, kinaesthetic – and reinforcing the valuable belief that their own observations, views, opinions and comments are valid.

Linking

One component of creative thinking is the ability to make links, because through making links one derives personal significance from anything and everything that happens in the world. In the context of education, what is taught may be learned; what is learned may be remembered and reiterated; but what is remembered will only become personally meaningful when it is linked with individual experience. As the educationalists Neil Postman and Charles Weingartner rightly assert in *Teaching as a Subversive Activity* **(see Bibliography, p.199) people are meaning-making machines. The process of education is and should be fundamentally a catalyst that allows this to happen.**

Linking is therefore a basic creative tool, and many of the activities in this book make use of it in a variety of ways.

Basic activity

In the context of the *Picture Discussion* game (p.19), select scenes from the *Picture Bank* (p.16) and:

- Invite students to make a list of as many ways of linking as they can.
- Assemble pictures to suggest storylines.
- Have individual students create picture sequences that carry personal meaning.
- Choose a sequence that somehow links members of the group (think of ten ways of doing this).
- Compile sequences that share moods, atmospheres, times, places...
- Collect pictures that are appropriate to a particular person, story, piece of music...
- Assemble pictures to create a montage that creates a powerful visual impression, or that illustrates an important theme or idea (the modern hi-tech world, human diversity, emotions, etc.).
- Match pictures with items from other resource banks.
- Pair a picture with an *Abstract Design* (see p.43).

The Tree

The tree template is a versatile device for presenting information, then accessing and reviewing it easily (e.g., see *Story Tree*, **p.168).**

Basic activity

To encourage students to develop the habit of using this technique, begin by drawing a treelike structure on the blackboard, then ask them what it could resemble, or remind them of: a river delta, cracks in rock, a nerve-network, etc.

Ask next what ideas could be presented by using the tree-shape. Give examples if suggestions aren't forthcoming: a family tree, the structure of an organisation, an overview of the systems in the human body, the way rumours might spread through a community such as the school.

Have groups research a favourite topic to see if they can present useful and interesting information by using the tree template. In one school where I worked, we actually made a sugar-paper tree that took up a whole wall. Groups in the class used the structure to link information in a chosen topic: major facts or themes were the big branches, subsidiary ideas formed the smaller branches, while individual pieces of information were written on paper 'leaves', and important understandings on pieces of 'fruit'. Every few weeks, we'd change the topic, re-labelling the branches and replacing the leaves. Some of the topics we enjoyed were: Dinosaurs, Space, Ancient Egypt / Greece / Rome, Science Fiction, Books and Films, Africa, Super-heroes, and Computers.

Brainstorming – a note on technique

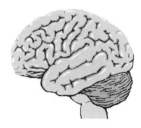

Brainstorming is and should be a social activity. It is also a very flexible one, ranging in its usefulness from being an ice-breaking game (Give me all the words you know that mean the same as 'big'), to a sophisticated and elegant way of exploring all of the implications of a hypothesis (Think of as many ways as possible of improving television sets so that watching programmes would be much more exciting and involving...).

Brainstorming is a pooling of ideas, facts, impressions, attitudes...Utilising the knowledge, imagination and outlook of each group member *as a resource*. Thus, it embodies a protocol which forms an integral part of the technique.

- All ideas are accepted and recorded. All ideas are equal.
- No one should offer any criticism of any idea at the generation stage.
- Every group member should be encouraged to contribute, though no pressure should be placed on anyone to do so.
- Encouragement should be given for participants to develop ideas already offered – so-called 'piggybacking'.
- No time limit should be placed on the session: it ends when the ideas run out.

Brainstorming remains a basic tool for stimulating creative thought, recognising and celebrating the idea that, as R.D. Laing once said, '*(personal) experience weaves meaning and fact into one seamless robe*'. In this context, the activity draws upon individual experience and *creates* an experience of its own, within which young creative thinkers find security through exploration.

Visualisation – Free Association, Guided Fantasy and Scripted Fantasy

A number of the techniques in this book rely upon what is usually called visualisation, which simply put, is the use of the imagination to create a mental picture. We all visualise much of the time, of course, but a few points can be made here to help exploit the ability.

To 'visualise' is to see something in the mind's eye. It's the most common way we imagine things, but not the only way. Look at an activity like *Ten Questions* (p.53) for example, to see how easily we can hear with the mind's ear, or touch with the mind's fingertips. The creative process is enhanced when more than one sensory modality of imagination is engaged – when we are as fully involved as possible with the scenario happening in our heads.

I have already indicated that one of the most powerful forces of the mind is 'meaning-making', of constructing a map of reality through the process of association. The cliché *'the world is what our thoughts make it'* expresses the idea precisely. Both the conscious and subconscious parts of the mind operate on the principle of significance: information coming into the mind, and actions resulting from decisions, will be placed within a 'hierarchy of importance' for our personal survival and well-being.

Daydreaming is a common and natural activity where the conscious point-of-attention swings inwards and, as it were, watches passively as the associative processes of the mind continue. Such daydreaming can be utilised and directed to increase the quality of creative thinking – by offering strategies that allow for the flexibility of individual thought within the structure of a classroom activity. Free association, and guided and scripted fantasy are examples of such strategies.

Free association is like the activity I've called *Constellations* (p.28), where random dots provide the structure within which individual creative thinking takes place. *Constellations* is a visual activity, but other sensory modalities could provide the emphasis (links between smells, textures, sounds).

The stereotypical free association activity asks participants to close their eyes or gaze at a blank surface. The group leader calls out single random words at, say, fifteen-second intervals, allowing each student to create individualized 'daydreams' which links the words in a meaningful way. By carefully choosing the list of words beforehand, the activity can be geared towards a particular theme or concept.

Guided fantasy is the next step on from free association. Here, to use the constellations analogy, the dots are chosen beforehand and the lines between them are already drawn. The nature of the activity is to allow participants to fill in the details for some predetermined purpose (or just for the fun of it!). Many of the story-making techniques in this book, such as *Story Tree* (p.168), make use of guided fantasy.

Scripted fantasy, as explained by Eric & Carol Hall and Alison Leech in *Scripted Fantasy In The Classroom* (see Bibliography, p.198), adds another layer of organisation to the imaginative process: here the dots are chosen, the lines are drawn, and the pictures are coloured-in beforehand. A good story, where the reader or listener becomes engrossed, is the ultimate scripted fantasy. Although activities such as *Deconstruction* (p.160) and *Dice Journey* (p.177) – especially if they are based on an extant novel or short story – employ all the useful functions of scripted fantasy in a way that allows participants a greater variety of active involvement.

Sometimes there is a certain apprehension about using these techniques because of possible controversial implications of the term 'fantasy' which children indulge in with their eyes closed, and the notion that daydreaming and education can't really have much in common anyway.

Obviously, as a teacher, you must use your own judgement in choosing whether or not to use such techniques. All I will say is that their ultimate purpose is to allow children to use *their* judgement more independently and profitably: and it seems to me preferable to have students daydreaming to some purpose, instead of just staring out of the window.

Eye Exercises

These safe and simple exercises refresh tired eyes and help to ease physical tension at the beginning or end of a sequence of *Imagine That...* games and activities.

Basic activities

1. For muscles that focus the lens.
Hold a finger up in front of your eyes and about two feet away from your face. Focus on the finger. Now focus on the wall beyond the finger. Now focus on the finger again...Alternate focusing on finger and wall about ten times.

2. For muscles controlling the size of the pupil (iris muscles).
Cup your hands over your eyes and count slowly to ten. Then take your hands away. During the count, the iris muscles relax, allowing the pupil to expand to compensate for the reduced light. Removing the hands increases the light input, so causing the iris to contract quickly. This exercise is good fun when working with a partner, who can observe the changes. Repeat three or four times.

3. For muscles controlling the movement of the eyeball.
a) Imagine a huge clock face painted on the wall opposite. Stare at the centre of the face. Twelve o'clock is located as high up as you can see by moving only your eyes (not your head). Three o'clock is at the extreme right, nine o'clock at the extreme left, and so on. Begin the exercise by moving the eyes to look at twelve o'clock. Every few seconds, move your eyes around the circumference of the clock face to the next cardinal point. When you have completed a clockwise circuit, repeat in the opposite direction.
b) Imagine a fly buzzing in the air in front of you. Follow its random movements for thirty seconds or so, then have it land somewhere and stare at it for ten seconds. Repeat a few times.

4. Palming.
Once you have completed the exercises above, rub your hands vigorously together and cup them over your open eyes for thirty seconds or so. This is a Yogic technique, which both soothes and refreshes the eyes. It can be used by itself, not necessarily in conjunction with the exercises described above.

Warm-up Games

There is an old saying, *Nothing worthwhile was ever accomplished without enthusiasm*. That enthusiasm is only forthcoming if the atmosphere, the ethos, of the session is right; and if the activities themselves promote meaningful learning-through-fun. What I call warm-up games set the ethos of the workshop, quickly and effectively.

Many of the activities in this book can be used as warm-up games, but here is a list of some old favourites...

- Draw a dot on the blackboard and invite ideas as to what it could be (see *Three Mexicans Weeing In a Well*, p.40)
- Ask for ten things you could use a paperclip for (or twenty or fifty things!)
- Play *What If* (p.86) as a quick-fire brainstorming game.
- Hold up some *Splash* cards (p.31) prepared earlier and ask what pictures can be imagined in them.
- Spend five minutes on the *Number Linking Dice Game* (p.26).
- Spend 10-15 minutes on *Artist and Instructor* (p.143).
- Use the *Sundries Bag* and have children describe objects detail by detail – 'It's rough, it's round, it's bigger than a grape but smaller than a plum...' Invite guesses from the rest of the group.

> "If you cannot find the truth
> right where you are, where else
> do you expect to find it?"
>
> *Dogen*

Section One

ASSOCIATION AND SEQUENCING

*L*earning may broadly be defined as a modification of thoughts, feelings and behaviours through experience. One of the main ways in which learning occurs is through the making of connections, and often sequential connections, between previously separate facts, ideas, objects, people, places and emotions – the emotional component being especially important, as this provides the 'glue' that allows the other elements of the learning experience to cohere positively or negatively in the mind. In this regard, and stating the obvious, if children come to associate learning with a sense of enjoyment, achievement, involvement and success, then a powerful positive feedback loop is established which will drive the whole process on into the future. Conversely, negative links with learning inhibit subsequent experiences and the eventual fulfilment of potentials.

This of course is using the concept of association in its widest sense. Links on the smaller scale provide the detailed 'stitching' that allows us over the years to create the entire tapestry – the big picture which becomes our adult perception of the world. That perception is what I have elsewhere called the 'map of reality', the blueprint that enables us to survive and at best to flourish in life. Much of this map, and most of our learning, occurs at a non-conscious level; which is to say that vast quantities of information are absorbed directly into the subconscious, where they are woven together as part of the meaning-making process that leads to an understanding of the world and our place within it.

It can truly be said, therefore, that we all know more than we think we know; and all of us are more than we believe ourselves to be. Tapping into this resource constitutes the engine that drives creative thinking. That engine can be 'oiled' through any activity that exploits and makes explicit our tendency to form associations. Such activities stimulate and strengthen our gift of insight, so that we come to learn with increasing clarity and power the truth of the adage – How do I know what I think until I see what I say?

Number Linking Dice Game

This activity can be used simply as an ice-breaker, or a warm-up before moving on to more elaborate games. Like many other activities in *Imagine That...*, this allows children to become involved in the process of having ideas that are not 'wrong', and that can be expressed, therefore, with confidence and enthusiasm.

Basic activity

The group sits in a circle. Spin the spinner to decide which student rolls the dice. When the total comes up, ask each child in turn to say what significance the number has for them.

E.g. The number 12 is rolled. Answers may include:

● There are 12 months in the year.
● My birthday is in December, the 12th month of the year.
● I am twelve years old.
● I have a pet dog and a brother who are both six years old.
● I have 12 pet goldfish.
    ... and so on.

Extension activities/ variations

● The game can go on to more subject-specific associations, for example, what is the significance of the number four in Geography (there are four compass points, four seasons etc.).

● Number linking using dice can be combined with other resources such as the *Sundries Bag* (p.17), *Picture Bank* or *Word Bank* (p.16). For example, if the number three comes up, the students take three objects from the *Sundries Bag*, three pictures from the *Picture Bank* and three words from the *Word Bank*. Collectively the students find as many links as they can between the three objects. Alternatively, try to find as many links as possible between the number three and each object, word, or picture.

● If you have two or more dice with coloured surfaces, you could explore links between colours. What links can be found between yellow, black and red, for example?

TIP

Always know in advance which activity is to follow on from number linking, and phase in gradually as soon as interest begins to wane.

Word Chain

GROUPING
Two or more teams

TIME
10-15 minutes

EQUIPMENT
Word bank, picture bank, dice

Word Chain is another game designed to allow children to have ideas spontaneously, to free them from the belief that they need to create and analyse at the same time. The activity demonstrates that having lots of ideas comes before selecting and developing the best ideas. In this sense, *Word Chain* is a useful precursor to more highly structured or elaborate thinking activities.

Basic activity

The activity leader draws a word at random from the *Word Bank* (p.16) and each team lists as many linked words as possible within a time limit (you could roll a dice to decide how many minutes to allow).

Extension activities/ variations

- As above, but now the teams must find a certain number of links within a set time (roll a dice to decide how many and how long).

- Choose two words and ask the teams to come up with a word or item which links the two. For example, what one word/item makes a valid link between *paper* and *happiness*? Some possible answers are: a thank-you letter, a five-pound note, my favourite comic, a drawing of a smiley face, a newspaper picture of someone who has won the lottery.

- Now choose a selection of words at random (see *Random Word Stimulus*, below), and ask teams to find suitable linking words, first to link pairs of words, then to link groups of three, four, five words and so on.

- Hand out a picture at random to each group and have the groups select words from the picture bank which can be linked with it. (Explain that groups should be prepared to explain their links later.)

- Ask the groups to create word chains. Each child in the group writes a word on a separate piece of paper. The groups then swap words and attempt to discover a linking theme within the chain.

- Hand out words at random from the *Word Bank*. Now give each group a theme word such as 'envy' or 'time'. Invite groups to forge links between the theme and as many of the words as possible.

Random Word Stimulus

A good way to generate words at random is to flip open a book and pick words off the page. Alternatively, you could play a story tape and pick every tenth word. Collect the words into a *Word Bank*.

Constellations

GROUPING

Individual work

TIME

10-15 minutes

EQUIPMENT

Paper, ink, ink sprayers (or photocopy the sheet opposite)

This is a simple visual association game. It is a useful way of generating ideas for creative thinking and writing since it bypasses the need for children to 'try' to come up with ideas consciously. Since the brain has a natural tendency to make patterns, plenty of ideas will come along quickly and easily.

Basic activity

Take a sheet of paper and spray dots over it. Photocopy the sheet and give a copy to each pupil. (Depending on time and resources, pupils could spray their own paper.) The aim of the game is to make new 'constellations' by seeing pictures or patterns in the dots.

Extension activities

● List the new constellations and ask the pupils to link the objects in a narrative. You could use storymaking activities such as *A Day In The Life* (p.131), *Story Tree* (p.168) or *Dice Journey* (p.177), to help create these narratives.

TIP

If children say they 'can't do it' draw a few lines between the dots to give them a start. Alternatively, suggest that children think of ideas under a heading – Insects, Shapes, Machines, Dinosaurs, etc.

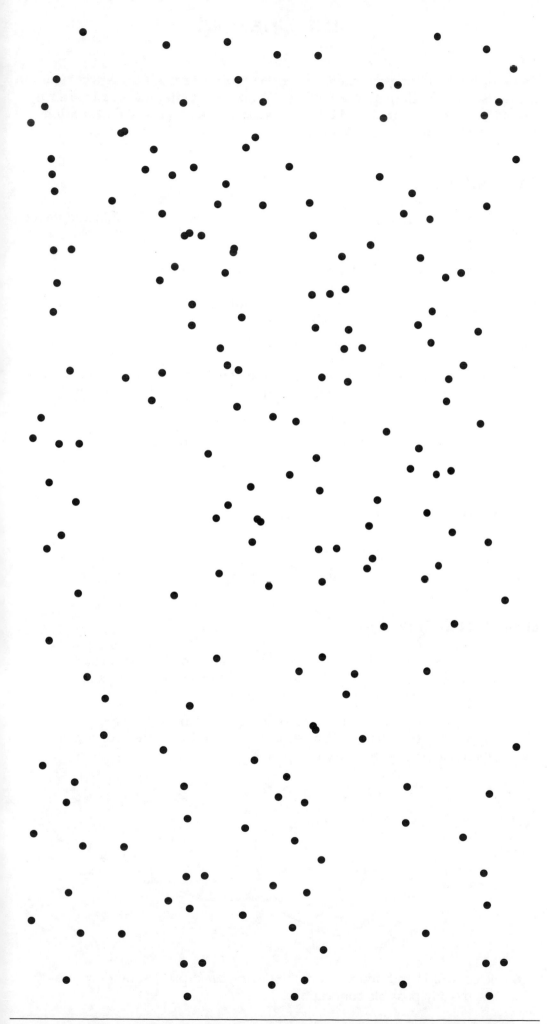

Odd-One-Out

GROUPING
Individual or pair work

TIME
20 minutes

EQUIPMENT
Word lists

Conventional odd-one-out exercises can be more a case of 'guess what's in the teacher's head', with many perfectly valid answers being marked incorrect simply because they are not the immediately obvious ones. This variation does something to redress the balance.

Basic activity

Present students with a number of groups of words which have a linked theme, such as:

1.	beech	elm	oak	violet	ash
2.	slate	gold	silver	iron	lead
3.	Glasgow	London	Berlin	Paris	Rome
4.	tea	coffee	biscuit	cocoa	orange juice
5.	baker	miner	tobacconist	draper	barber

Briefly play 'guess the right answer' (1. violet – not a tree; 2. slate – not a metal; 3. Glasgow – not a national capital; 4. biscuit – not a drink; 5. miner – not a 'seller'.)

Now ask groups to devise 'right' answers for every other item in each of the lists.

Extension activities/ variations

- Find links between all the items in a list.
- Devise other, more difficult odd-one-outs.

Linked activities

- Use any of the words in a list and link it with a proverb or piece of wise advice. E.g. Oak – 'Great oaks from little acorns grow'. Now follow the instructions given for *Confucius-He-Say* (p.148).
- Use words from any of the lists to 'hang' on branches of a *Story Tree* template (p.169). These then become seeds around which ideas grow when that part of the story is explored.

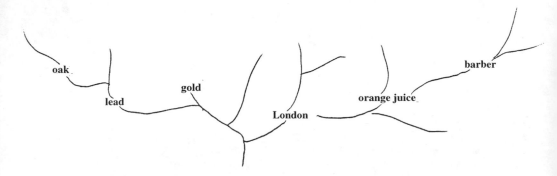

- Select words and images from the *Picture Bank* (p.16) at random and discuss any possible connections.

Splash

Eloquent arguments have been advanced that the ability to see patterns is hard-wired into the human brain. *Splash*, based on the Inkblot Test devised by psychologist Hermann Rorshach, is a simple association exercise which exploits this idea (although it has no psychoanalytical overtones).

Basic activity

Students flick, sprinkle or smear inks or paints onto sheets of paper, then fold the paper over to create an inkblot.

Discuss each of the inkblots and invite students to offer interpretations. The abstract images could then be used to provide a stimulus for story-making.

Linked activities

● Combine the exercise with other techniques described in the book, such as *Free Association* and *Guided Fantasy* (p.21) in order to extend and enhance the ways in which children become sensitive to pattern and detail, similarities and differences; and to allow them to realise that all too often in the world of creative thinking, answers are not 'right' or 'wrong', only 'more, or less, useful'.

NOTE

An interesting sidelight on the theme of *Splash* can be found in the idea of the simulacrum, or 'shadowy likeness'; the tendency to see figures and faces in random abstracts of light and shade. John Michell's book *Simulacra* (see Bibliography, p.198), is full of such images. These are ideal as the basis of discussion, fantasy or ghost stories, investigations into folklore and legend etc. Within areas of science, these images could be used to aid work on optical illusions such as the so-called 'Mars Face', Percival Lowell's Martian Canals, animal mimicry, and so on.

GROUPING Individual or small group

TIME 20 minutes

EQUIPMENT Paper, paints or inks, painting tools

Picture Sequences

GROUPING

Groups of 4 or more

TIME

20-30 minutes

EQUIPMENT

Selection of pictures from magazines, picture bank, etc.

This activity draws together many of the mental skills employed in creative thinking: observation, assimilation, deduction and extrapolation, within the framework of having lots of ideas before you can select the best/most useful ones.

Picture Sequences can be combined with other thinking games and targeted at specific areas of the curriculum:

- English/Drama – use to build narrative structures
- Art – use as a stimulus for individual or group artwork and design
- Music – combine picture sequences with appropriate pieces of music which share a similar theme or mood
- History/Geography – collect pictures which reflect a certain historical period or geographical location. Or collect pictures which trace routes of, say, a grain of rice from where it is grown to the dinner plate.

Basic activity

Students take pictures form the *Picture Bank* (p.16) and assemble them in particular ways, or according to certain themes. For example, they could place the pictures in order of:

- dramatic content
- action and movement
- degree of mood or atmosphere
- attractiveness of subject
- degree of realism
- degree of fantasy
- degree of ambiguity
- personal preference (compare and contrast within the group)
- importance of theme
- personal associations

Extension activities/ variations

- Ask students to add to the above list by suggesting other ways in which the pictures could be grouped.

- Hold a debate in order to reach a consensus of opinion across the whole class about which is the most attractive picture, fantastical scene, important theme etc. Discuss what qualities determine attractiveness, drama, importance. Can we ever be objective about such things?

Relationships

This activity makes use of the resource bank materials (see pp.15-18) to stimulate creative thinking, and forms a preliminary exercise to more complex and sophisticated games.

Basic activity

Students take two pictures at random from the *Picture Bank* and discuss possible relationships between the people and/or scenes shown in the two images. E.g.:

Annabelle: These two people are brothers because they look alike – they both have the same shape face and similar smiles. Both of them look well-off. This man is dressed in a suit so I think he's a business executive. This other man is more casual but still smart-looking. It's his day off. They're arranging a golf match...

Peter: I think this lady would feel sorry for the man in the picture with her because he looks dirty and miserable. I think she's his social worker. This other picture of the countryside is where the man grew up... He wants to go back there. That's his dream.

> **NOTE** Remember to explain to groups that, in association exercises, there are no right or wrong answers but that the links they suggest do need to be justified.

Extension activities/ variations

Draw more pictures from the *Picture Bank* to increase the complexity of the relationships network

Linked activities

● *Circles* (p. 47). This game can be used to make further investigations into relationships: to add detail to the relationships between two or more people in a picture; to gather ideas about the relationship that exists between nations, or between a geographical area and the people who live there; to explore the impact of scientific discovery or invention upon society. You could also use the *Relationships* idea on a selection of pictures of animals. Follow up by using the *Circles* template (p.47) to add detail and sophistication to ecological ideas.

GROUPING Small groups (4-6)

TIME 15-30 minutes

EQUIPMENT Picture Bank (p.16)

Acronym

GROUPING

Small groups

TIME

15 minutes

EQUIPMENT

None

This is a good kick-start exercise which is lots of fun. Use it to make children familiar with brainstorming – having lots of ideas before they can select the best ones.

Acronyms are also handy for remembering some useful ideas.

What	Trying	Work
I	Is	Is
Really	Better	Play
Mean	Than	
Is	Winning	

Basic activity

Take an acronym – e.g. UFO – and ask students to think of as many things as possible that it could stand for.

Extension activities/ variations

Now ask students to:

● adapt one acronym to make others – UFO – IFO – OFO – BFO – and, again, think of as many things as possible that they could stand for.

● make up sentences using longer acronyms. E.g. UNICEF – Under Nightly Instructions Cows Engineer Fireworks.

● Take someone's name as an acronym to sum up his/her personal qualities...

Smiling

Tries hard

Energetic

Very thoughtful

Excellent effort

(Acronyms make excellent badges if you have access to a badge-making machine.)

Themed Acrostic

Themed Acrostic is an excellent way of gathering ideas for stories and it can also be used as a technique for brainstorming.

Choose a word appropriate to the theme of a story (alternatively, students could choose words which interest them). Now ask students to think of linked words that begin with each letter of the chosen word. E.g.:

Andromedan attacks in an anguished advance. Alien anatomy.

Long, lizard-like lifeform leaps.

Inter-planetary interloper, insidious, insectile.

Earth endangered by enemy engineering.

Nemesis comes at night.

This, and the example below, are also kennings. A *kenning* is an ancient poetic form which combines description with action, as in the following example.

Fast flyer

Airborne acrobat

Lighting striker

Clawed killer

On-the-wing stalker

Never-quit predator

Morpho

This is a visual variation of the old word game Ladders, which involves taking a 'start word' and an 'end word', and gradually turning one into the other (e.g. CAT... COT... DOT... DOG), though *Morpho* has more scope for creativity. It can be used as a warm-up activity.

Basic activity

1. Ask students to draw a series of between 4 and 10 rectangles on a sheet of paper and number them.

2. Next, have them think of a simple image (e.g. a cat) and draw it in the first box.

3. Ask them to write the name of another simple image that will be drawn in the final box (e.g. a boy.)

4. Students now exchange papers. The task is to fill the intervening rectangles with a series of more-or-less meaningful drawings that slowly transform the object in box one into the 'target' object in the final box.

A Cat 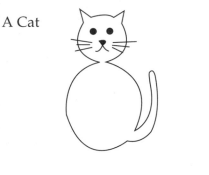 A Boy

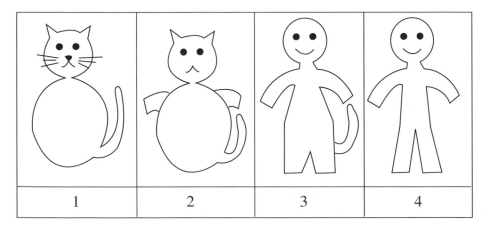

| 1 | 2 | 3 | 4 |

GROUPING

Pairs

TIME

20 minutes

EQUIPMENT

None

Invent-A-Word

Invent-a-Word **puts to one side rules and conventions of language and encourages instead an attitude of enthusiasm, independence of thought, and a playfulness towards words. It is an easy and fun activity which can be played at any level. The objective of the activity, as the title implies, is to create new words. The aim is to create a** *sense* **of language, where the emphasis is on language as a process to be enjoyed rather than a product to be judged.**

Basic activity

Focus first on the purpose for which the new word is required – the job it has to do. It could name something, describe something, identify an action – for example, a new kind of dinosaur or machine, a strange animal of custom, a new game. Look at several words which already do the same job in other contexts to see if there are any common features (from which rules can subsequently be derived – e.g. *ing* endings on action words, words that can be names or descriptions – such as colour words, red or blue). Encourage students to experiment with lots of ideas, discuss choices with classmates and be prepared to make changes. Suggest that they:

- play with the order of letters in the new word
- consider word endings
- think about onomatopoeia, rhyme and rhythm (nursery rhymes are often good examples)

Linked activities

- You could use the above activity to invent a name for a creature based on *Footprints* (p.66). You could then go on to create the rest of the creature and put it in an environment. What sounds does it make? Invent words for features in its imaginary world and other creatures there.

To take this further, you could have creatures go on a *Dice Journey* (p.177), through their imaginary landscape. Ask students to devise new words for the discoveries they make on their travels.

 Create a resource bank of the newly invented words for use in other activities.

Brainwave

GROUPING	Whole class or groups
TIME	10-15 minutes
EQUIPMENT	None

This is a discussion game using brainstorming principles to develop skills in assessing a subject and collectively drawing conclusions.

Basic activity

First of all decide on a topic for consideration, such as 'lunch'. As a whole class or in groups, have students consider different aspects of the topic – e.g., food, timing of meals, junk food, irradiation, school meals, convenience food, etc.

Allow 5-10 minutes for ideas to be accumulated, then ask students to consolidate them, discuss issues separately and in more detail, and finally, draw up a list of conclusions/recommendations.

Possible Topics

> The Perfect Town
> New School Rules
> Designing a Zoo
> A Better Kind of Transport (than cars)
> The House of the Future

Try to make sure that the tone remains positive and objective so that the activity does not degenerate into a general moan about school dinners (or whatever).

A core principle of brainstorming is that contributors don't judge ideas initially, but simply generate them.

Grabbit

GROUPING | Whole class

TIME | 20 minutes

EQUIPMENT | None

This game illustrates the rules of brainstorming in a fun way by encouraging an 'anything goes' approach to the generation and accumulation of ideas. *Grabbit* sessions should be fast, furious, noisy and brief. They differ from other brainstorming sessions in that they allow other questions and hypotheses to grow out of the initial question. What results is a spray of ideas that can be simply enjoyed as they emerge, or be subsequently reviewed, assessed and developed.

Basic activity

Put forward a hypothesis – e.g. suddenly scientists are able to grow tomatoes as big as footballs – and ask students to speak out the ideas/consequences/questions that come to mind. E.g.:

- Bamboo garden canes would need to be replaced by steel girders.
- You'd need really big slices of bread for your sandwiches.
- Can scientists already do this?
- Tomato sauce would be cheaper because you'd have bigger tomatoes.
- Could you make all fruit and vegetables bigger?
  etc...

Possible Topics

Water becomes very scarce
Somebody actually learns how to create dinosaurs
A huge computer suddenly becomes intelligent
Unexpectedly, everyone in the world loses the power of speech

TIP | Once thinking becomes hesitant, self-conscious or silly (because the children have run out of ideas), or hypercritical, the game is ended.

Linked activities

- *Grabbit* bears a close resemblance to *What If?* (p.86) but differs in the way in which suppositions are tackled. *What If?* can be used as a warm-up game, but in its fully developed form calls for thoughtful and detailed speculation on a group theme. *Grabbit* demands off-the-cuff responses which add fuel to the fire of group creativity.

Three Mexicans Weeing In A Well

GROUPING

Whole class or small group

TIME

20 minutes

EQUIPMENT

None

The Creativity Consultant Roger Van Oech tells a wonderful story in his book *A Whack on the Side of the Head* **(see Bibliography p.199). His English teacher put a chalk dot on the blackboard and asked the class what it was. After a few seconds someone said "It's a chalk dot," and everyone sighed with relief that the obvious had been stated. The teacher pointed out that the day before she had put a similar dot on the blackboard in front of a kindergarten class, and the five-year-olds spontaneously and enthusiastically – had come up with fifty ideas of what the dot might be. Von Oech makes the point that 'hardening of the categories' had occurred in the ten-year interval between kindergarten and high school.**

Part of the problem is that children are not encouraged to think divergently within a supportive atmosphere. Most thinking, as Edward de Bono points out in *Teaching Your Child to Think* (see Bibliography, p.197) is reactive thinking; a simple response to information received, often based on an exaggerated concern for getting the 'right' answer. The chalk dot technique celebrates and practises the notion that students themselves can generate answers, often in ways which are startlingly effective and powerful because they are personally meaningful.

Three Mexicans Weeing in a Well is an extension of the chalk dot game.

Basic activity

Draw this image on the blackboard and ask "What's this?".

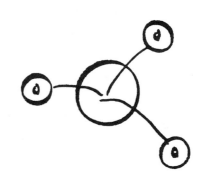

Extention activities/ variations

● Ask each student to think of, say, another six things that the above image could be.

● Design another six shapes and ask the class what they could be.

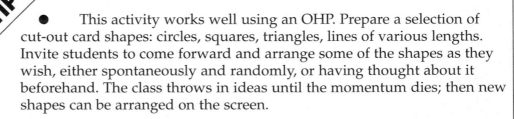

TIP

● This activity works well using an OHP. Prepare a selection of cut-out card shapes: circles, squares, triangles, lines of various lengths. Invite students to come forward and arrange some of the shapes as they wish, either spontaneously and randomly, or having thought about it beforehand. The class throws in ideas until the momentum dies; then new shapes can be arranged on the screen.

● Try directing the activity along thematic lines. Put up a heading – e.g. The Future – and encourage students to link the shapes with that theme.

Comic Book Cut-Outs

This is a basic sequencing activity that's great fun. It gives children a greater insight into how story-making works, by developing their sense of narrative structures and highlighting the fact that stories can follow many potential paths. Individual picture frames are used to serve the same purpose as a *Context Sentence* (p.90), allowing children to ask the big, open questions of When?/Where?/ Who?/ Why?/ What?/ How? before they begin sequencing events. In order to justify a chosen sequence, children will also have needed to think about the purpose and motivations of the characters.

Basic activity

Cut out pictures from comic strip stories and ask students to reassemble the stories from clues given by each picture.

Extension activities/ variations

- Mix up pictures from different stories and/or using different comic characters and ask students to arrange them in a meaningful sequence.

- Present students with a comic book story from which one or more pictures have been removed. Ask students to discuss what the missing pictures depict, what dialogue is being spoken, etc.

- Give students a few pictures from a story and ask them to supply the missing sections of the story.

- Give students one picture from the middle of a story and have them discuss what happened up to that point, and what happens next.

- The idea of comic book characters can be used as the basis for all kinds of creative work: inventing new ones, redesigning costumes for superheroes, transposing superheroes into different genres, designing secret bases for comic characters, and so on.

Linked activities

- Incorporate comic strip pictures with *Story Tree* (p.168) to explore a range of narrative possibilities.

- Use frames from comic book stories to help guide *Dice Journeys* (p.177).

- Comic strip pictures can also be used as a stimulus for *Picture Discussed* (p.19), *Circles* (p.47), *A Day in the Life* (p.131) and other activities that require a visual focus.

Abstract Art

This is a simple visual association game, similar in principle to *Splash* (p.31), *Symbols* (p.45), *Morpho* (p.36) and join-the-dots type activities.

Basic activity

Give each group a sheet showing an abstract art design. These could be prepared and photocopied beforehand or created by students themselves from a few simple guidelines:

- Use only simple geometrical shapes such as circles, triangles, straight and wavy lines, ovals, etc.
- Don't have any particular object in mind as you make the drawing.

Ask groups to discuss what the pictures represent. Encourage a range of interpretations for each card.

Extension activities/ variations

- Have groups create meaningful sequences of abstract art cards.

Linked activities

- Abstract art cards could be helpful as prompts to the imagination in activities such as *Dice Journey* (p.177) and *Story Tree* (p.168).

GROUPING Small groups

TIME 20-30 minutes

EQUIPMENT Abstract art template (p.44)

TIP If no ideas come spontaneously turn the picture upside down!

Symbols

Symbolism is a testament to human creativity and a wonderful example of the inherent complexity of often simple-seeming forms. Symbols themselves represent a visual shorthand that is expressed in most areas of human activity.

This exercise examines the everyday use of symbolism and its function.

Basic activity

Begin by asking groups to think through a number of curriculum areas and note where symbols are used (e.g.: Maths – +, -, %; chemical formulae in Science; weather symbols in Geography, etc...). Now ask them to look at areas where they aren't used and either work out why they are not, or try to invent symbols that would be appropriate.

Encourage groups to consider symbolism in familiar areas such as heraldry, media imagery, computer icons, company logos etc., and explore the breadth of symbolic expression – from religious iconography to the workaday practicality of roadsigns.

Extension activities/ variations

- Select a basic shape such as a circle and brainstorm what it could represent; firstly without making any changes to it, then by removing/repositioning portions of the circumference; and then by adding subsidiary shapes.
- Use other familiar images for the same purpose: a hand, an eye, a series of dots, a sword, etc.
- Take an heraldic symbol and encourage students to discuss its overall design, and also what particular features might mean. (Explaining what the symbols *actually* mean is an optional extra.)
- Have groups or individuals design a coat-of-arms representing themselves, the class, the year group, the community.
- Design a personal logo.
- Redesign the school logo.
- Design symbols to represent emotions, abstract ideas, etc.
- Invent symbols to represent the spirit of the Millennium.
- Create new 'roadsigns' for a colony on the Moon or Mars.

Colour Spiders/ Design a Flag

This activity can be used as part of *Symbols* work. Ask groups to use spider diagrams/key word plans (association clusters) that link ideas pertinent to particular colours. Most common colours are rich in meaning as the example on page 46 shows.

Groups can now discuss their colour links and bear them in mind as they design flags to represent new countries or express their personal views of existing countries.

GROUPING	Whole class or small group
TIME	30 minutes
EQUIPMENT	Books from different curriculum areas

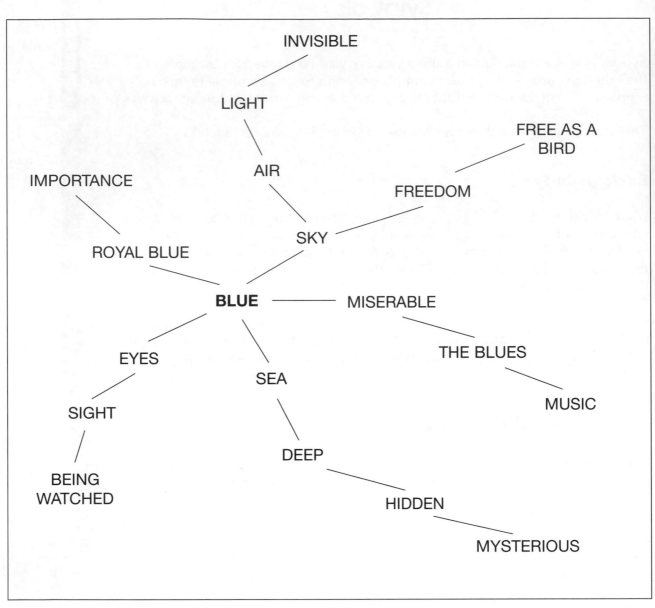

Spidergram for the colour Blue

Circles

GROUPING Small group

TIME 20-30 minutes

EQUIPMENT Circles template

This activity involves a technique which I developed for encouraging students to think about character development in creative writing workshops. Within 15 minutes or so it is possible to flesh out a complete personality in terms of physical attributes, internal forces and psychological factors, important life events, general background history, and that character's relationship with other characters (who can also be generated by the same method).

Basic activity

First draw on the blackboard a series of circles similar to that shown below.

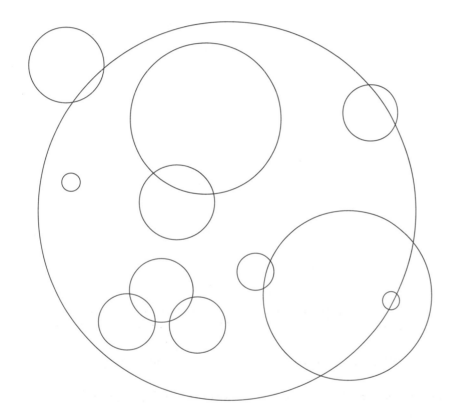

Explain to the class that:
- The large circle represents the whole personality. Anything beyond the large circle can be seen from the outside – a visible feature or behaviour particular to the character being created.

- Anything inside the large circle goes on within the person – it could be something physiological, or thoughts, emotions, drives, dreams, fears etc. The size of the circles indicates the importance of whatever they represent. If circles overlap, then whatever they represent must be linked in some way – maybe in terms of what the character needs, wants, believes, and so on.

Now ask the class for ideas about what the circles might represent (you could choose from the selection either by agreement through discussion, or by rolling a dice). Use the dice to determine how intelligent the character is, how good/evil, etc. (a dice roll of 1 = hardly at all; a dice roll of 6 = extremely).

Extension activities/ variations

You can also use the linked circles device to:

- Represent the elements of a story. Take a well-known and fairly simple story, such as *Little Red Riding Hood*. The large circle represents the whole story; everything beyond it is the 'real world'. The other circles might represent issues and themes within the story, such as Red Riding Hood's concern for her sick grandmother, the woods as an element of the story, the wolf as a character in the story and a symbol of threat, Grandma's fate, the woodman as a rescuing-hero character, etc.

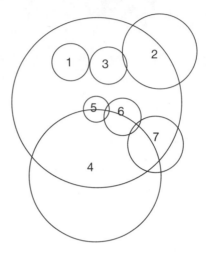

- Explore the ecology of a rain forest.

- Represent events happening at a certain time and place. (The circles represent a town. The big circle is the town boundary; the smaller circles are things of greater or lesser importance happening in the town right now... As events take their course in the town, the positions and sizes of the inner and outer circles will change.)

- Create character maps for real people: yourself, family, friends, famous personalities.

You can also use the overlapping circle device in other ways:

- 2-3 circles – explore similarities between yourself and your friends.
- 6 circles – explore thematic overlaps between genres in literature, art, music etc.
- 10 circles – explore friendship/acquaintanceship groups.
- 10 circles – explore the influences on your life.

Cross Match

Creative thinking often involves finding connections where none existed before. At the most sophisticated level such insights are supported by years of experience and a vast knowledge of the subject. But the habit needs to start somewhere. Most often it happens naturally and spontaneously, when a child picks up a stick and it becomes a raygun or sword, or where she sees patterns in the clouds, or where the box a toy came out of is more interesting to play with than the toy itself...

Cross Match helps to encourage the habit of creative cross-connection.

GROUPING Small group

TIME 20 minutes

EQUIPMENT Polyhedral dice

Basic activity

Take a number of headings and list items under each heading. E.g.:

Profession	Machine	Fruit or vegetable	Transport
1. Doctor 5. Lawyer 9. Shopkeeper etc....	2. Drill 6. Digger 10. Food mixer	3. Orange 7. Potato 11. Carrot	4. Car 8. Bus 12. Train

Number the items so that a (polyhedral) dice can be used to introduce the random factor if required. Now cross-match items in each list in a number of ways to see what you get. For example, what do you get if you cross (dice roll: 1) a doctor with (dice roll: 3) an orange? Any answers are acceptable – from 'a doctor with an orange car' to ' a doctor who thinks vitamin C cures colds' to 'his name is Dr. Orange.'

Extension activities/ variations

● Choose two categories (e.g. fruit and machine) and a letter of the alphabet. Ask students to create descriptions starting with the chosen letter – e.g. a Juicy Jaguar, a Fruity Fiat, a Squishy Sierra.

Linked activities

● Take any cross match and create a *Spidergram* (p.46) to extend into broader themes – e.g. Machine cross matched with fruit or vegetable may lead you into... organic systems ... environmental friendliness... house plants to control heat...humidity and oxygen in the home...etc.

● Use cross matches as the basis for a *Story Tree* (p.168) or *Parallel World* game (p.92).

Section Two

FIVE SENSES FOCUSING

*T*here is an ancient story about a man who was wandering through the countryside. He was intent on reaching his destination, and didn't really pay much attention to whatever was around him. He failed, therefore, to notice the tiger that had been stalking him for some time, and which now sprang out of hiding to chase him.

Startled and frightened, the man dropped his baggage and ran as fast as possible away from the tiger. As he ran, however, he was dismayed to realise that his path was taking him directly towards the edge of a cliff. There was no time to slow down, no other direction to take – and so the man jumped over the brink.

Luckily, he was able to grab hold of a small bush growing right on the edge. He glanced up at the tiger looming over him licking its lips, thinking that perhaps it would go away soon, and that it might not be such a bad day after all...

Just then, the roots of the bush began to tear free of the crumbly rock of the cliff. With a gasp, the man glanced down to see how far he was going to fall – only to catch sight of the tiger's mate waiting below for the clever trap to be sprung.

In his final moments, and rather unexpectedly, the man noticed a clump of strawberry plants sprouting close by. On impulse, he picked an especially plump and ripe-looking strawberry, sniffed it, then popped it whole into his mouth.

How sweet it tasted!

I love this story, partly for its wonderful wry quality, but also because it illustrates a couple of highly significant points.

Think about some of your own learning experiences, and you may soon come to realise that the power and 'educational effectiveness' of the experience is largely dependent upon the state of your emotions at the time. The way we feel textures the content of our learning, negatively, neutrally, positively, and also adds a vital component to the meaning we make from what we encounter.

Equally significant is the realisation that we all have the capacity to use our own senses more powerfully to help in the meaning-making progress. Whenever the world seems bland or uninteresting, it is because of the way we are, not the way the world is. Our ability to notice is always present while we are awake, and that ability can be refined and developed in many ways, and to great effect, as the following activities hopefully show...

Five-Senses Focusing

GROUPING

Whole class

TIME

30 minutes

EQUIPMENT

Sundries bag

This is a basic awareness game which begins to establish the useful habit of directed attention. It has many variations, and can act as a precursor to most of the other activities in this book.

Basic activity

Ask students to sit quietly and become aware of the sounds occurring nearby, moving perhaps from the loudest to the softest, or from those closest to those furthest away.

Now ask the students to *imagine* what other sounds exist around the school, or change the group's mind's-eye picture by getting them to think of sounds at home, in a city, in a wood etc.

Extension activities/ variations

- Use the *Sundries Bag* (p.17) to direct the children's attention towards textures, then have them imagine the textures of various things, perhaps by combining this with language work – perhaps using *Word Banks* (p.16).

NOTE   Focusing on shape, size and colour – the visual aspects of an actual or imagined environment – can lead easily towards the kind of guided fantasy work described in the next activity, and is the most powerful application of this activity, since most information we receive directly about the world is visual.

Some example questions

- What does milk look like as it is poured into coffee or tea?
- What does a fire sound like when sticks are put on it?
- What is your favourite taste? Describe it as exactly as you can.
- What do sugar crystals look like?
- Imagine plunging your hands into a bucket of flour. What does that feel like?
- What does petrol smell like? (Describe the smell, not whether you like it or not.)
- Imagine you are a seagull taking off from a cliff top. What are your feelings?
- What are the *exact* colours of the eyes of a person sitting nearby?
- Touch the back of your hand. What does it feel like?
- You are in a parked car by yourself. It's raining heavily. What sound does the rain make on the car's roof? (Do not use obvious words like pitter-patter, splish-splash, etc.)

Ten Questions

GROUPING Whole class

TIME 20 minutes

EQUIPMENT None

This is a basic concentration/visualisation activity in which students are asked to focus their attention on imagined sights, sounds, smells, scenarios, etc. The activity helps to develop the component skills of creative thinking, but also forms a mental tool in its own right. For students to be able to step into the narrative imaginatively via a number of senses sharpens their perception and clarifies the detail of the scene.

Basic activity

A typical sequence, allowing plenty of scope for free choice, might run as follows:

"Close your eyes now, or stare at a blank surface, and concentrate on the following..... Gather your thoughts to create an impression of a place. Any place will do – somewhere you're very familiar with, or perhaps a place you know only vaguely, but would like to visit; or just let your imagination come up with something to surprise you. When you have a basic impression of this place where you imagine yourself to be, become aware of the following...

1. What is nearby? Just look ahead and notice something in front of you.

2. What colours do you see?

3. Begin to turn around and become aware of other things, some close by and some far away. What are they?

4. Turn your attention now more towards the sounds you find in this place where you imagine yourself to be. What do you hear? Pick out at least three quite separate and different sounds.

5. In your mind, reach out and touch something. What does it feel like? Now contrast this by feeling other surfaces, paying attention to the different textures you find.

6. Let yourself relax a little more and begin to notice the smells and aromas in this place where you are. Don't struggle to identify these smells, just let them come and give each one a name or a description: sweet, sour, fruity, etc. What is the most distinct smell in your imagination?

7. Now pay more attention to anything that's moving in this place. What are the different kinds of movement you can see? If nothing is moving, do something about it: make things move, even if only a little.

8. Is it warm or cool where you are? After you've noticed this, go in search of something that's cold. Touch it and feel the coldness. Now find a different something that's hot. Are you able to feel what's cold with one hand and what's hot with the other, at the same time?

9. Now look around for something you can pick up. Hold it in your hands and become aware of its weight, how warm or cool it is; how rough or smooth. Notice the colours and all the little details of this object. Fix them in your mind...

10. Now change your point-of-view so that you're looking at your imagined place in a different way; from high up or low down, from directly above, or imagine that you are very small. What do you notice that's different now?

It's time to leave the place where you've been. Over the next few moments, bring your attention back to the here-and-now. I hope you've enjoyed your journey..."

Extension activities/ variations

● Focus attention much more specifically. For example:
"Imagine you're standing on a beach, on wet sand. There are some pebbles of various colours lying at your feet. Pick up three pebbles of different colours. Feel the weight and size and texture of those pebbles. Notice some little gritty sand grains clinging to the pebbles. Brush them off so the pebbles are perfectly smooth.

"Pick your favourite pebble of the three and drop the others. Look closely at the colour or colours of your chosen pebble as you become aware of the great variety of shades in the stone. Bring the pebble up to your mouth, stick out your tongue and touch the pebble with its tip to taste the salt.

"Now put the pebble in your pocket as you take a look around you. Notice what's moving: the sea; perhaps grass on the dunes blowing in the breeze; perhaps some seagulls. Notice how the waves come up on to the beach... It's a shingle beach further down; millions of pebbles rattling together as the waves splash over them and the water drains back down with the outgoing tide."

And so on...

● Another way of using the fine-focusing attention technique is to set the scene, focus the attention, then ask a question to select a modality and elicit an individual response....
"You're on a shingle beach. There are millions of pebbles reaching as far as you can see. Notice how the waves come crashing up over the stones, before the water drains back to the shoreline. Listen to the sound of the water running through those pebbles? What sound do you hear? What does the sound remind you of?"

Linked activities

● Ten questions work can be used to add depth to *Point-of-View* exercises (see Section Five), linked with areas of study in History, Geography, and Science by putting yourself, imaginatively, into a particular time or place. E.g. you go back to the time the pyramids were built in ancient Egypt.

TIP
A good source of scripted fantasy ideas can be found in *Scripted Fantasy in the Classroom*, by Hall, Hall and Leech (see Bibliography. p.198).

Sound Journeys

GROUPING — Whole class

TIME — 30 minutes

EQUIPMENT — Tape of sounds previously recorded

This activity builds on devices like *Ten Questions* (p.53) and other visualisations. The broad aims of this activity are to exploit the existing mental preferences of 'auditory thinkers' (a great deal of classroom work favours visual thinking) and to develop the confidence and ease-of-use of 'sound thinking' in children whose preference may be to imagine visually or kinaesthetically. Practising this and related activities expands the mental toolkit and allows children to think from a broader base.

Basic activity

Prepare a tape of sequenced sound effects. Ask students to close their eyes or stare at a blank surface and visualise the objects that are causing the sounds.

Now go on to run one or all of the activities below.

Extension activities/ variations

- Ask groups to take a short story or parable, and create a sequence of sounds that act as a backdrop to the narrative. Alternatively, have students create sound sequences (without voices) that sum up particular parables. Other groups then attempt to match the sound sequences to the parables.

- Have students match sounds on tape to their written (onomatopoeic) equivalent (you may already have suitable cards in the *word bank* (see p.16); if not, have children devise them as part of the exercise).

- Use individual sounds to help children imagine, then draw or build a Heath Robinson-style machine. (p.78)

Linked activities

- Use random sounds as part of a *Free Association* exercise (p.21). Choose a sound initially to allow students to locate themselves in an imagined place. Encourage them to let their thoughts wander (remember, this is a creative daydreaming!), and either allow this to continue for a few minutes, then feedback, or offer further sounds each minute or so, to provide 'hooks' for their thoughts.

- Collect sounds that are thematically linked. Taking the theme of 'time', a visual display of onomatopoeic words, or an audio tape, might include the tick-tocking of clocks, the chimes of Big Ben, an owl hooting, a cock crowing, traffic at rush hour, the rattle of milk bottles as a float passes by, and so on. This is an auditory equivalent of a *Theme Card* (p.17).

- Combine sound sequences with *Map-Maker* (p.80). If you are constructing and imaginatively exploring, say a woodland, use the sounds of birds, animals, the wind in trees, etc. to enrich the creative experience.

- Use sounds in *Dice Journeys* (p.177) or *Circles* (p.47), or to inform decisions in *Story Tree* (p.168) – 'Should we explore this old house by turning left or right at the end of the corridor?' Play two sounds at random – the first hinting at what's left, the other at what's right...

The Spice Trail

GROUPING
Whole class, pairs or small groups

TIME
30 minutes

EQUIPMENT
Spices

This activity, like many others in the book, is designed to raise awareness, in this case of the landscape of tastes and aromas. Ask students to bring in interesting or unusual items which can be tasted or smelt – obviously, within guidelines that have been set down beforehand! – or prepare a 'spice journey' yourself with some carefully chosen samples.

Basic activity

Children can either work in pairs, small groups, or as whole class. One child is put in charge of the aromatic items; the others in the group are asked to close their eyes or gaze at a blank space, and not to compare impressions yet. Spices, herbs and/or other aromatic items are offered one at a time. Children sniff for a few seconds, then write down their impressions. These can include:

● guessing what the spice actually is
● recording what the smell reminds the children of (which may have no immediate or obvious connection with the item itself)
● noting differences/ similarities with other aromas

Extension activities/ variations

There are many other things you can do in this activity:

● Describe tastes and smells in as much detail as possible. Distinguish between the taste/ smell itself and students' reaction to it ("This is gross" is an opinion, not a description).

● Make creative comparisons – "If this smell could represent a colour/ animal/ place/ machine/ person, etc., what would it be?" You could also work this the other way round by choosing an object and selecting a smell to represent it.

● Compare two similar tastes as precisely as possible, noting differences between the taste of peanut and cashew nut, for example.

Linked activities

● Use flavours and smells as components in creative games such as *Dice Journey* (p.177). Give children the opportunity of sampling aromas during the story-making as a stimulus for further ideas. As you circulate amongst groups, ask children what the character in a story can smell at that point. A similar approach can be taken during discussions in *Picture Discussion* (p.19) and as an enrichment component in *Story Tree* (p.168).

● Use smells and tastes as sensory triggers in memory enhancement. (See *Cosmic Memory*, Ostrander and Schroeder, Bibliography p.199) for more details – the basic principle is that if you have the smell of, for instance pine in the air when you study, it is easier to recall that information later if the same smell is present.)

 Check carefully with regard to food allergies and related conditions before running this activity.

Sounds of Silence

GROUPING	Whole class
TIME	20 minutes
EQUIPMENT	None

People often say you don't notice the tick of a clock until it stops. *Sounds of Silence* exploits that phenomenon to focus attention upon the diversity of sounds we experience; our dependency upon them, and yet the fact that we take them entirely for granted.

Basic activity

The basic activity is a 'noticing exercise' to allow children to understand what other components, apart from the voice, are involved in communication. This can take the form of watching the TV with the sound turned off, pointing out that we 'get the message across' by the way we stand, our gestures, the facial expressions we use, and so on.

Develop the idea by having a 'no voice' slot in a lesson. This could take the form of a game of Charades (where children mime the title of a book, film, etc.), or of attempting to communicate an idea visually, e.g. that the planets go round the Sun, which is at the centre of our solar system.

Extension activities/ variations

- Ask groups to tell a story without sound, using mime, pictures, etc.
- Have students pretend they are sales people: their task is to sell a product without the use of sound.
- Use a collage, or sequence of video clips, slides, pictures, or other visual material to form a visual journey or create a particular atmosphere.

Sensory Stimulus

In my workshops I use all kinds of ways to try and stimulate creative thinking; the cross-matching of ideas with a flexible structure that allows those ideas to evolve. As a broad principle, engaging the different senses in the creative process enhances interest and motivation, and thus creativity. And once the idea is established, many novel variations can be found.

Basic activity

Take three short pieces of music (or three tastes, smells, or textures). Tell the group that the first piece of music (or whatever) is a person, the second is a place, the third is an event. Play them through and ask students simply to listen without making any special effort, and to jot down any ideas that come to mind.

Now, instead of using just music to evoke a sense of person, place or event, use different sensory stimuli to achieve the same purpose. Ask children to imagine a piece of music as a person, a smell as an event (e.g. "The smell of jam reminds me of the time we went on a picnic and an inquisitive sheep wandered over to see what we were doing..."), and a place as a texture (e.g. "This sand reminds me of a very windy weekend we spent at the seaside. It felt gritty in my hair and on my teeth...")

	Person	Place	Event
Taste	X		
Smell			X
Texture		X	

The aim of this exercise is to open up the way children consciously and deliberately notice the world through their different senses, and then use their heightened sensory acuity to make imaginative links with areas of thought they are asked to explore.

Extension activities/ variations

● Another way of running the exercise is to take a place, character or event as part of a story-making game and to select a piece of music that defines and represents it. So, find a person that has the texture of sandpaper (not literally!); or a place that reminds you of the flavour of apricots. Use pictures and other resource bank material as an aid.

● Try cross-linking two senses in a novel way: find a texture that represents, say, the colour purple; or a colour that you could say has a bitter taste.

● Use colours/ textures/ tastes and smells to suggest words and/or dialogue. Choose, say, verbs, and prepare a dozen different textures. What verb does each texture suggest? Or select *particular* verbs and ask students to match them with the textures.

Linked activities

- Explore cross-linking two senses by having children mix colours in an activity such as *Splash* (p.31) and see if the resulting picture suggests any kind of music to them, or a particular character (if so, the character could be fleshed out using *Circles* (p.47) or *Character Cards* (p.117) as templates.

- Look at *Emotion Spectrum* (p.132) and try to link different emotions with colours (easy), then smells (not so easy), music (easy), and then textures (more difficult).

- Ask students to create colour abstracts that help to define a mood or an emotion. Or create a 'sensory collage' to express an emotion, or spirit of a place (see *Inscape*, p.68), or a character – either an archetypal figure, or a particular individual. The material generated could be used as the focus of descriptive work to evoke a sense of atmosphere and place in a *Dice Journey* (p.177) or to encourage directions to explore in a *Story Tree* (p.168), or to help construct rationales and explanations in the *Mythologies* exercise (p.161). In all of these cases, the abstract nature of the raw material – a smell, a piece of music, a blend of colours – creates a structure, a potential, within which children have the flexibility to make creative links.

Soundtrack

GROUPING	Whole class, small group is or individual work
TIME	30 minutes
EQUIPMENT	Video or audio cassettes and players

Watching television is often criticised as being a passive activity, where children uncritically absorb someone else's highly designed representation of the world. *Soundtrack* is one way of involving children actively in a pastime most of them enjoy, in a way that stimulates their imagination and develops their ability to observe and extrapolate creatively.

Basic activity

Tape a short piece of dialogue from radio or television (a few minutes will be be plenty). Ask groups to:

● speculate on what the speakers look like, and from there, what they are like as people
● discuss what led up to the dialogue clip, and what happens afterwards
● from what people say in the dialogue, decide what their larger environment is like
● discuss the hidden thoughts behind what is said in the dialogue (people often say one thing but think another)
● discuss the use of tone, pitch, volume and other qualities of the voice in the dialogue
● discuss what body language may be going on between characters during dialogue.

Explore the ideas in group discussion (small groups or whole class). The ideas and impressions which have been generated can then be incorporated into other activities or form the basis of extension work....

Extension activities/ variations

● Use music soundtracks and/or special effects noises to create different storylines from the one/s suggested by the dialogue clips.

Linked activities

● You could use the taped dialogue in the same way as for *Context Sentences* (p.90). Listen again to the TV dialogue and note down any unanswered questions that occur to you.

● Use music and/or sound effects with paragraphs taken from stories (published text, or students' own work), and use these as the point where you would 'step into the story' in a *Dice Journey* (p.177). The material can be used to encourage observations (of time, place, character) and speculations about what's happening so far, and what could happen next.

Section Three

OBSERVATION & DEDUCTION

Some years ago I went through a Sherlock Holmes phase. I bought omnibus editions of Conan Doyle's Holmes novels and short stories, and read the lot. They were thoroughly enjoyable, but have since faded into a general impression of the world of Sherlock Holmes. Apart from two memorable exceptions...

Having visited the great detective hundreds of times in his rooms at 221b Baker Street, Watson happens to wonder how Holmes manages to come up with his brilliant deductions which allow him in the end to crack the crime or solve the deepest mystery. By way of reply, Holmes asks Watson how many stairs he has to climb to reach the room where they are now having this conversation. Watson has no answer to give.

'You have climbed those stairs almost as often as I have, Watson,' Holmes replies in so many words. 'And I can tell you there are thirteen of them. And there, I suppose, lies the difference between us.'

The other scene I remember is where Holmes mentions the strange occurrence of the dog barking in the night. 'There was no dog barking in the night,' Watson points out. ' That,' says Holmes, 'is the strange occurrence.'

Our capacity to notice things would be of little benefit if we did not then go on to make use of the details we observe. And by 'making use' I mean to construct meanings that allow us to survive and to flourish. Sherlock Holmes was renowned for his powers of 'deductive reasoning'. It sounds like a very intellectually-based skill, but the process also goes on in the human mind at a non-conscious level. Our conscious perceptions (i.e., what we observe and deduce from that) inform the subconscious map of reality, which in turn supports the conscious meanings we derive from the world around us. It is an endless feedback loop which incorporates all the new information that comes our way, moment by moment.

This process happens anyway, but we can learn to do it better. And since reading Doyle's books, I have come to believe that if we combine our conscious abilities to observe and deduce with our more non-consciously based intuitions and insights, we become most empowered as learners.

Red Lorry Yellow Lorry

GROUPING	Pairs or individaul work
TIME	5-10 minutes, or over lunch time, or set as homework
EQUIPMENT	None

This is a simple observation game. Perhaps in the past you've realised that as soon as you've noticed, say, a woman in a blue hat, lots of women are wearing blue hats. This is because our attention is usually very selective. In psychology the rule is that, at any one time, we tend to notice seven items plus-or-minus two. In other words, most of the world goes by without our being aware of it!

Basic activity

Ask students to write down an ordinary, everyday item – a blue hat, a red pencil, the word *and*, or whatever. Put all of these suggestions into a bag and draw one out. Pairs of students (or individuals) then have a certain time in which to notice the target item. Each pair keeps a tally, perhaps with notes of any variations – blue hat with black ribbon, dark blue hat, blue velvet hat, and so on.

Description

This broadly based activity highlights the idea that even the simplest object embodies a great complexity. Description games hone language and observation skills, and help develop the habit of taking the next step beyond the obvious. Noticing, and commenting upon what one has noticed, is a cornerstone of many subjects – and there is therefore a direct link between discussing a face in a picture chosen from the *Picture Bank* (p.16), and assembling observations of a scientific experiment.

Close description of objects is a good warm-up game or time-filler.

Basic activity

Pick items from the *Sundries Bag* (p.17) and ask individuals or groups to describe them in as much detail as possible. Direct attention where necessary to other sensory modalities (e.g., what sound does the object make if you tap it with a pencil?) and encourage students to move towards greater detail (what *kind of* 'rough' is this object?).

Extension activities/ variations

● Hand groups two pennies and ask them to notice any differences between the coins. (I usually suggest that children try to spot six differences, but the record currently stands at 19!). Encourage children to describe differences too – e.g. rather than just saying the Queen's hairstyle is different, describe *how* it is different.

GROUPING Pair work or small groups (up to four)

TIME 10-15 minutes

EQUIPMENT Assorted objects gathered in advance

Masking Pictures

GROUPING

Whole class (with OHP picture) or small groups

TIME

20 minutes

EQUIPMENT

Prepared masked pictures, OHP

This is a standard exercise in Media Studies, but has wider applications in the field of creative thinking. Link it in with other picture work and with other activities such as *Elementary, My Dear Watson* (p.77), as described below.

Basic activity

Take a picture and prepare photocopied versions where different portions have been masked off. Ask groups to discuss what they can see of their portion, and what might be happening `beyond the frame'. Opinions and value-judgements are permitted, because one purpose of the activity is to show how readily we all form opinions based on partial evidence.

Now ask groups to relate to each other what they think is going on in the picture – before revealing the picture in its entirety. Discuss what led groups or individuals to form their initial opinions.

Extension activities/ variations

- Give groups whole pictures and ask them to prepare a number of card or paper masks to block out portions of the picture so that various interpretations of it become possible.

- Hand out different masked pictures to the work-groups, together with a range of captions or 'headlines', and have students match picture-with-caption, again with the aim in mind of showing how, through the media and our own partial perspectives, our views of the world are engineered.

- Link this activity with writing or drama. Ask groups to invent scenarios, parts of which are then written out or acted. After discussion and speculation about 'what's going on', the rest of the scene is presented.

Follow up by looking at the whole issue of value-judgements, bias, prejudice, etc.

Linked activities

You could go on to play *Elementary My Dear Watson* (p.77), another activity which encourages observation followed by extrapolation.

If...Then

This works well as a warm-up game, and helps to define the ethos of a creative environment. The activity seeks to stimulate quick-fire spontaneous responses to hypothetical questions.

If...Then is similar to *What If?* (p.86) but seeks more explicit and logical connections between the stimulus question and the children's response. The difference is one of emphasis.

Basic activity

Tell the class that in a few moments you will give them an *If...Then* hypothesis. Explain that they have a time limit of, say, two minutes in which to suggest as many consequences as possible. After two minutes, give another *If...Then* stimulus. Some examples are:

- If trees could talk, then....
- If the stars came out just once in a hundred years, then...
- If pigs could fly, then...
- If promises had to be kept, then...
- If we were one inch tall, then...
- If we changed colour according to our emotions (green with envy, etc.), then...
- If we had a TV remote control that worked on people, then...
- If time was a videotape, then...
- If we could stop time,then...
- If Father Christmas really existed, then...

No judgements should be made about the quality of the answers and no follow-up work need be done.

GROUPING
Whole class or small groups, if ideas are to be discussed

TIME
15 minutes (for whole class exercise).

EQUIPMENT
None

Footprints

GROUPING

Pairs

TIME

30 minutes

EQUIPMENT

Footprints
template (p.67)

A useful way into this activity might be to explain how the principles of deductive reasoning are applied to many areas of research: a palaeontologist reconstructing an extinct animal from fossilised fragments or ground traces; an archaeologist fleshing out the dynamics of a vanished culture from shards and splinters; a detective piecing together a chain of events from disconnected items of evidence.

Footprints introduces these ideas, but can also be used with many other activities in this book for a range of other purposes.

Basic activity

Prepare a number of footprint sheets beforehand. These can either be based on real creatures (there are many books on animal tracks and trails), or constructed with imaginary beasts in mind, such as the examples which follow. Now ask the class to speculate on what the whole creature might look like, and how it might behave, based on the footprint evidence.

Make it clear from the outset that speculation must be based on what can actually be seen in the picture ("But Darren, how do you know this monster has got four purple tentacles and six eyes?").

The game can also feature tracks left by machines.

Linked activities

Footprints links well with *Picture Bank* (p.16), *Theme Acrostic* (p.35), *Invent – A – Word* (p.37), *One Unique Detail* (p.70). *Life But Not As We Know It* (p.79) and *Map Maker* (p.80).

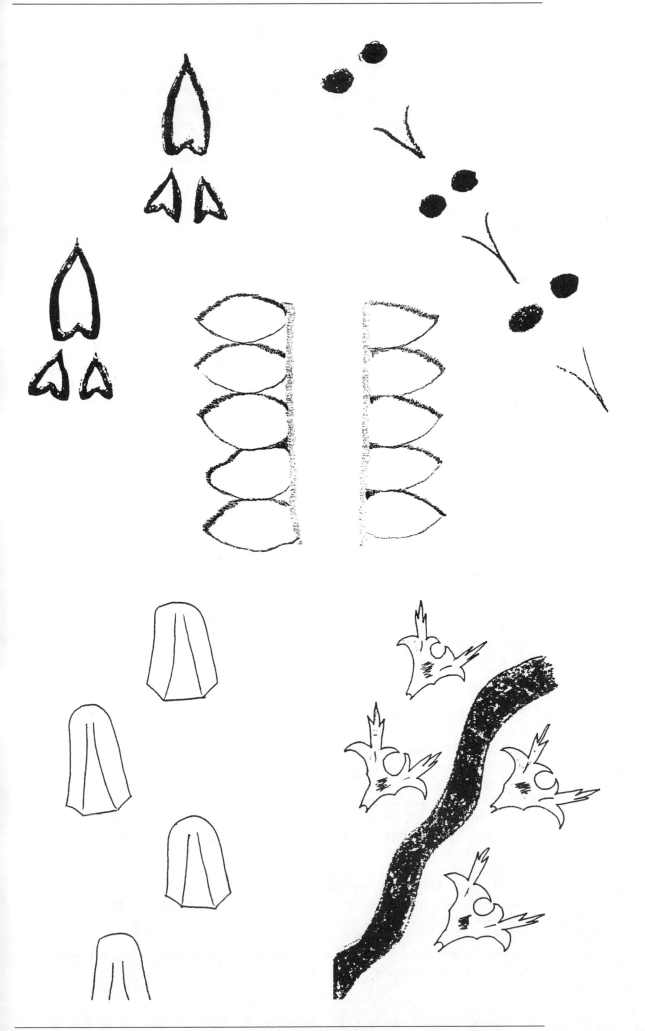

Inscape

Inscape **combines observation and discussion with the development of a sensitivity towards the uniqueness of things. The term was coined by the Victorian poet Gerard Manley Hopkins to describe the individual nature and distinctiveness of all created objects. His endeavours to express that individuality and its energy of being (which he called 'instress') resulted in some of the most beautiful and skilfully crafted poetry ever written.**

At the very least, *Inscape* is about noticing, and appreciating, differences on an increasingly subtle scale.

Basic activity

Ask students to choose an object and describe one feature of it as exactly as possible, avoiding obvious words and clichés.

As a brief example of how the technique can work... During one workshop, I asked students to describe the exact colour or colours of the eyes of someone sitting nearby. A minute or so later, one boy put his hand up and grinned. "Sir, John's just put 'blue'!"

"Whose eyes are blue, John?"

John pointed to the boy next to him and looked sullen. I went over and looked at the lad's eyes. Yes, they were blue.

"John, look around and pick out at least six different shades of blue. Which one matches most closely the colour of your friend's eyes?"

"Sir, he's not my friend. I'm just sitting by him..."

"OK. Which blue matches?"

John pointed to a calendar picture of some trees and a field.

"Yes, John, that's a really good match. Now, 'blue' is just a name in this case, and not a description; so let's work on that. What time of day do you think this picture was taken?"

"I dunno."

"Look at the shadows."

"Um, they're short, so..."

"So the sun's quite high up?"

"Yeah."

"Right, would you prefer it to be morning or afternoon in that picture?"

"What? It doesn't matter."

"Of course it does. Just choose – or we could roll the dice to decide."

John smiled. "It's afternoon."

"Early afternoon, because the sun is high... Now what time of year do you think the picture was taken?"

"Er...The leaves on the trees are mainly green, but some are going yellow... And in the field, the crop has been harvested: it's stubble – hasn't been ploughed back yet."

"Right. So?"

"Well, how about early September?"

"Fine. So this boy's eyes aren't just blue... They're the blue of an early September afternoon sky."

"That sounds really soppy."

"Yes, but it says more than 'blue' – and it's just a first attempt. You need to have lots of ideas before you can pick out your best ones."

Extension activities/ variations

● Assemble pairs of similar objects and have students talk about the differences.

● Look at synonyms and ask why we bother to have words that 'mean the same thing'.

● Take two obviously different items (a leaf and a stone; a Muslim and a Christian) and ask students to discuss what the similarities are.

● Ask why today is different from any other day.

● Ask students to list (privately if they wish) why they are unique in the world (see also *One Unique Detail*, p.70 and *Positive Self Image*, p.112).

NOTE

Remind the students to choose exact descriptions, while avoiding pedantry of course.

One Unique Detail

This activity can be run as an exercise on its own or as a follow-on from *Inscape* (p.68). It was devised as an aid to generating characters in creative writing workshops.

Basic activities

One Unique Detail can be used in many ways:

- Ask students to think about 'OUD' with regard to themselves. It could be an external detail, or something inside. E.g.:
  Dave – "My one unique detail is the little scar on my left knee, where I fell over when I was six."
  Ellen – "The iris of my right eye is definitely greener than my left."
  Harinder – "My one unique detail is me!"

- Have individuals look at each other, or pictures of people in search of OUD. E.g.:
  Aaron – "I think Susie's one unique detail is that her dog, Toby, will only bring sticks back to her, and no one else!"
  Jai – "The man in this picture looks very unhappy even though he seems to own a big house... Is this unique?"

- When students write stories, use the OUD device to `tag` minor characters, and to act as an introduction to major figures.

- Apply the OUD idea to other objects, events and concepts. Encourage it as an attitude-of-looking at the world.

GROUPING

Individual or pair work

TIME

15-20 minutes, including time to note observations

EQUIPMENT

None

Freeze-frame

GROUPING Small groups or whole class

TIME Up to 30 minutes

EQUIPMENT Extract from story

This activity develops the observation and extrapolation skills targeted in previous activities, while giving children the confidence to gather and express their ideas within a structure of open questioning of text. A whole-class run-through could then be followed by groups of children working independently on further paragraphs.

Basic activity

Take a paragraph at random from a story, making sure it is interesting and can sustain the degree of questioning which is to follow. Either allow students to know from which portion of the story (introduction, middle, end) the paragraph came – though without telling them which story it is; or dice-roll on a 1-6 scale to determine its place in a hypothetical narrative (1 represents the beginning of the story, 3 the middle and 6 the end – so a dice roll of 4 dictates that the chosen paragraph should come after the middle of the story); or say nothing about the extract.

Extract:

The noise was deafening. There was a huge roar and great clouds of orange dust rolled up to meet them.
Together Tim and Teena ran towards the only shelter, under the platform. There they crouched while rocks banged and clanged on metal, and soil poured around their ankles.

from **Dinosaur Day***. Bowkett S (Heinemann Banana Books, 1996)*

Now ask the students to think about the questions that the paragraph throws up – about things such as who the characters are, why they are behaving in the way they are, who is telling the story, what has led up to this point in the story, etc. E.g.:

- Where might Tim and Teena be?
- What could have happened to bring them there?
- Who are Tim and Teena?
- What is the platform?
- What might happen next?

Once a context has been explored, ask students, working alone, in pairs or small groups, to firm up their ideas by sketching out a possible storyline (see example on p.72). This need only be a few lines long, although you may wish to develop it into a more substantial piece of work.

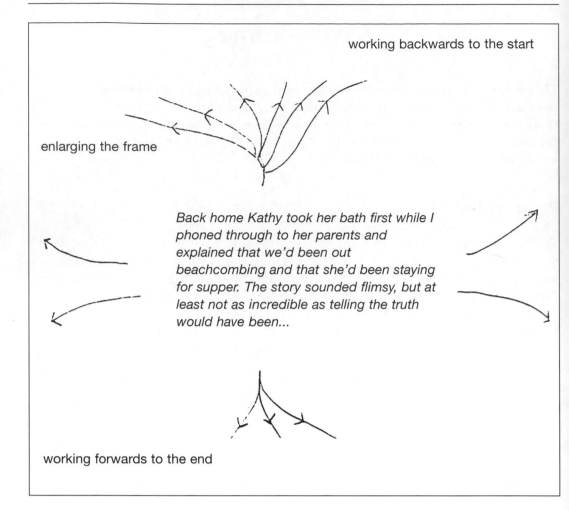

working backwards to the start

enlarging the frame

Back home Kathy took her bath first while I phoned through to her parents and explained that we'd been out beachcombing and that she'd been staying for supper. The story sounded flimsy, but at least not as incredible as telling the truth would have been...

working forwards to the end

Linked activities

- *Picture Sequences* (p.32). Use visuals chosen from the *Picture Bank* (p.16) to give focus to a storyline being developed.

- *Dice Journey* (p.177) can be employed to explore narrative possibilities, working outwards from the original paragraph.

- *Context Sentences* (p.90) would be an effective preliminary exercise to get students in the mood for *Freeze-frame*.

- *Deconstruction* (p.160) might usefully follow the creation of storylines based on *Freeze-frame*. This would allow students to become aware of the wider thematic base of any stories they have created.

Habitat

Habitat is another context-type game which encourages students to look beneath the surface when presented with material – a sentence from a story, a picture, a statement about someone, a judgement or a generalisation. Such activities aim to change the habit of jumping to conclusions in the absence of evidence or prior thought. Useful conclusions are always informed, and in this climate one common conclusion is 'there's not enough information to decide'.

Basic activity

Collect a range of pictures or written descriptions of 'habitats'. First of all, using the idea loosely, ask students to comment on the type of person / animal / community / culture / race that lives there, together with a justification for those observations.

As the activity unfolds, discussion is likely to range across many subject boundaries: Geography, Biology, Sociology, Psychology; and accommodate ideas such as stereotyping, pop culture, prejudice, the meanings of words, advertising and persuasion.

The game can be played in two ways: either by revealing 'the right answer' once discussion has occurred (which will, more often than not, reveal how many false assumptions the group has jumped to), or leaving conclusions speculative, but making the point that what we decide about people, places, events and so on is often based as much upon what we don't know as what we do.

Linked activities

- *Footprints* (p.66). After playing this game, devise a habitat within which the hypothetical animal might live.

- After playing *Habitat*, invent dialogue for your made-up people to speak. Use pictures of pairs of eyes to speculate on what they might be thinking. (This is *Elementary My Dear Watson* (p.77) played in reverse.)

- *Inscape* (p.68); *One Unique Detail* (p.70). Use the central concept of these games to speculate on specific details when you devise a habitat. This counters the tendency to generalise, and also fixes created habitats more firmly in the imagination. Inscape examines why any certain place is unique in a broad sense. Take two streets the children know – how are they different? 'OUD' picks out a single unique item. 'My street is unique because....'

GROUPING Whole class or small group

TIME 30 minutes

EQUIPMENT Pictures of habitats

Chilli Chicken Stir-fry

GROUPING

Whole class

TIME

30 minutes

EQUIPMENT

Utensils and ingredients as detailed

During our 'options afternoon' at a school where I worked, I taught stir fry and curry cookery – which gave me the idea for the following activity.

One way of highlighting the concept of interdependency (in this case with regard to trade and economy) is to take a common recipe and see where all the ingredients come from.

Basic activity

Choose a recipe that requires a wide range of ingredients and utensils and buy or borrow the items that are needed. In the case of the stir-fry recipe for chilli chicken, all of the food items were bought from just two shops, a local supermarket and a Chinese grocers.

Now ask the group to discover in which country each of the ingredients and utensils was produced.

eggs, chicken, celery, shallots – Britain
green pepper – Spain
red pepper – Holland
root ginger – Costa Rica
chilli sauce – Thailand
soy sauce – China
sesame seeds, sesame oil – Singapore
corn oil – USA
cornflour – USA
rice – Pakistan...
kitchen roll, dishcloth, kitchen knife – Britain
cutlery – Korea
bowls – Japan
scissors – Italy
wok – China

Pin a large map of the world on the wall and tag the locations for all of the items used in the recipe, ingredients and utensils.

NOTE
You have to decide where to draw the line as this exercise could go on and on. Where is the cooker made? Where does the wood come from that makes up the kitchen units. It is also interesting to acknowledge that behind every object lies an industry – in fact, a network of industries: manufacturing; transport; communications. The web is endless.

Extension activities/ variations

This idea and method of display can be used if students investigate where their clothes come from, or the various items in their rooms at home.

Chilli Chicken Stir-fry – Recipe

Ingredients:

350 gms chicken breast meat, skinned and shredded

1 tsp cornflour

4 tsp corn oil

2 shallots, cut into lengths of 2-3 cms

1 slice (or more to taste) of fresh root ginger, shredded

1 small red pepper, 1 small green pepper, cored, seeded and cut into pieces

2 celery sticks, sliced or cut into matchstick shapes

1 tbsp soy sauce

2 tsp chilli sauce (or more to taste)

few drops of sesame oil

1 tsp white wine vinegar (optional)

sugar to taste (but not more than 1 tsp)

Method:

1. Put shredded chicken into a bowl with salt and cornflour, mix and leave to stand for 20 minutes.
2. Heat 2 tbsp of corn oil in a wok until very hot, and stir-fry chicken for about 2 minutes over a moderate to high heat (keep it all moving to avoid burning). Remove and drain. Set aside.
3. Heat remaining oil and add shallots, ginger, peppers and celery. Stir-fry briefly (so vegetables are hot and crunchy).
4. Add soy sauce, chilli sauce and sesame oil (and wine vinegar / sugar if using).
5. Return chicken to wok, heat thoroughly and serve with plain boiled rice.

(Makes two generous or four measly portions)

Timelines

GROUPING

Whole class initially, splitting into small groups

TIME

20-30 minutes

EQUIPMENT

Timeline (photocopied or OHP)

One function of science fiction is to predict the future; environmentally, technologically, politically, and so on. The purpose of *Timelines* is not necessarily to attempt an accurate and detailed sweep of future possibilities, but to engage in the act of creative anticipation. This can be targeted towards specific subject areas and themes – global warming, the fate of the African elephant, computers, medical progress – or it might reflect the personal viewpoint or hoped-for future of the individual.

Basic activity

1. Draw a vertical axis and mark off sections a couple of centimetres apart, which represent gaps of a year or five years or ten years, etc. Put the current year at the base of the timeline.
2. Choose which areas of speculation you want to work on – space travel, developments in computers, ecological issues, or whatever (preferably something that is likely to develop dramatically in the future).
3. Use the timeline both to focus students' thinking, to introduce concepts relevant to the area of enquiry, and to note down ideas generated.

E.g.   A timeline focusing on space exploration

2050 – First Martian colony established

2040 – First lunar colony established

2030 – Multinational manned mission to Mars

2020 – Unmanned European probe lands on Titan

2010 – First unmanned probe reaches Pluto

2002 – New Space Station launched as an international project

Linked activities

The activity might also be incorporated into character-generation work and *Dice Journey* (p.177), to pin more detail to an invented world or person.

Elementary, My Dear Watson

GROUPING Small groups

TIME 30-40 minutes

EQUIPMENT Samples of taped/written dialogue to cut up, selections from the Picture Bank (p.16).

This is a basic observation and deduction game which develops the skills of noticing details, and speculating in a reasoned way to reach conclusions based upon what is observed. It is a more focused activity than pure brainstorming.

Basic activity

This activity can take several forms.

- Listen to a short piece of taped or written dialogue. Ask the students to speculate on the personalities and backgrounds of people, represented only by dialogue.
- Cut out pictures of clothes from a catalogue and discuss the kinds of people that might wear them.
- Use pictures of pairs of eyes to deduce what might be going on inside the head of the person depicted.
- Pick words at random from the *Word Bank* (p.16) and use them to create associations pertinent to different character types.

Extension activities/ variations

A variation of the game is to invent scenarios which present a puzzle. Players then use deductive reasoning to solve the puzzle. For example:

- A man is found hanging in a locked room. There is no furniture beneath him or nearby – no stool kicked away, etc.; but a large damp patch can be seen on the carpet below the hanged man. Account for the circumstances of his death?

  Answer: The Man committed suicide by standing on a block of ice until it melted.

- Jack and Jill are dead! They are found lying on the floor with pieces of broken glass and splashes of water around them. A sash window looking out over the garden is open by just a few inches, but the door to the room is locked from the outside. How did Jack and Jill die?

  Answer: Jack and Jill are Goldfish. Scamp the Cat knocked their bowl off the floor.

Ambiguous Objects

GROUPING

Small groups

TIME

20-30 minutes

EQUIPMENT

Items brought in by students and/or collected previously by the teacher

This game consists of swapping items, or pictures of items, whose function is not immediately apparent. It develops skills of observation and speculation with a particular emphasis on how structure is related to function.

Basic activity

Collect a range of ambiguous-looking items or pictures of items. Give one to each group and ask them to attempt to work out what the ambiguous objects might be used for. A simple example might be to show a group, say, a slightly unusual piece of kitchen equipment such as the kind of steamer made of 'petals' that folds up to enclose food, and then ask what this item could possibly be used for. (Ask anyone who actually knows what the object is for, to keep quiet while others try to guess.) Guide ideas by pointing out particulars of how the object is constructed.

Thinking styles will vary. Some students will approach the activity logically and methodically: others will rely on a spray of ideas that can be evaluated later. Needless to say, any student can benefit from the way another deals with the task, such cross-fertilisation forming an essential component of the activity's aims.

Linked activities

● Use *Five Senses Focusing* (p.52) to encourage children to explore ambiguous objects with all of their senses as they speculate on its function.

● *Three Mexicans Weeing In A Well* (p.40) can act as a warm-up to *Ambiguous Objects,* inviting the class to look at an ambiguous object from different perspectives.

● Incorporate *Ambiguous Objects* with *Elementary My Dear Watson* (p.77) by inserting an obscure object into a scenario as part of a puzzle (see *EMDW* extension activities). For example, why was the kitchen steamer found in a garage amongst tools for repairing an engine?

Heath Robinson

A variation of the game is to show students a number of Heath Robinson designs, then invite them to devise mechanisms of their own to carry out some simple task. (See Bibliography p.197)

Life, But Not As We Know It

This game illustrates the relationships between structure and function with particular emphasis on living creatures.

Basic activities

Begin by thinking about existing creatures and how their design helps them to live in their environment. Why is a giraffe's neck so long? Why do ducks have webbed feet? Why do snakes have backward-pointing fangs? Ask students to look at the way that human beings are built, and to suggest reasons for our form... Why do we have two eyes and ears high up rather than low down? Why do we have hair on our heads? Why do our thumbs stick out from the sides of our hands?

Now ask students to design a new creature, either to occupy a particular environment on Earth, or a planet in outer space whose basic climatic conditions have been discussed earlier; or a creature that serves a particular purpose for humanity.

The depth and sophistication of the activity can be varied according to the age and abilities of the students and/or the particular educational aims the group leader has in mind. There is certainly scope in *Life, But Not As We Know It* to explore ethical questions of genetic engineering, for example, or ecological/environmental issues.

Extension activities/ variations

Focus the activity on machines rather than creatures (this activity can be combined with the *Heath Robinson* game described on p.78).

NOTE

The following books contain material that may be helpful for this activity (see Bibliography, p.197 for more details).

- Dougal Dixon, *Man After Man* illustrates how human beings may continue to evolve far into the future

- Dougal Dixon, *The New Dinosaurs* asks 'What if dinosaurs had not become extinct, but continued to evolve right up to the present day?'

- The CD-ROM *SimLife – The Genetic Playground*, (published by Maxis, 1995). This is a fairly sophisticated educationally based computer game that invites users to program certain factors into ecological scenarios in order to see the outcomes. New kinds of animals can also be created by a mix-and-match process.

- Dorling Kindersley's *Eyewitness Guides* in book or CD-ROM format provide excellent backup for this activity, together with superb visuals.

GROUPING Whole class initially, then small groups

TIME 30 minutes for individual projects. Development work could span several lessons

EQUIPMENT See Note

Map Maker

GROUPING
Whole class (using OHP demo) and/or small groups

TIME
30 minutes upwards

EQUIPMENT
Ordnace Survey, or 'home-made' maps

This game allows students to become familiar with OS map symbols and the way these can be translated within the imagination into features of the landscape. More generally, *Map Maker* develops powers of observation and deduction as the map fragments are placed in a wider context.

Basic activity

Begin by cutting a large scale map into pieces – 127x76mm is a good size – and pasting them on to larger sheets of blank paper.

- Have groups speculate on what geographical features lie beyond the map segment.
- Ask students to draw or describe what they can see from particular vantage points, both on the map extract and beyond the frame.
- Ask groups to take certain features of their map and combine them with another group's selection to create a new landscape.
- Think of different names for villages and towns on the map.
- Supply lists of standard map symbols and have students design their own landscapes.
- Supply students with a small portion of an OS map (perhaps with the rest masked off) and ask them to fill in the missing areas.

Linked activities

- Use map segments for story making (see Section Seven), free association and guided fantasy, etc.

- Use 'home made' landscapes or OS maps to help design creatures in *Life, But Not As We Know It* (p.79), or machines to traverse those landscapes.

- In conjunction with *Symbols* work (p.45), ask students to invent new map symbols and icons.

- Use landscapes from the *Picture Bank* (p.16) as a starting point for landscape design.

- Focus on landscapes (designed or supplied) as backgrounds in story making activities such as *Story Tree* (p.168) and *Dice Journey* (p.177).

- Use maps in point-of-view work, visualisation and guided fantasy exercises.

Plan-A-Journey

GROUPING Small group

TIME 15-30 minutes

EQUIPMENT Maps, atlases, dictionaries

I always had a map of the world on the wall in my classroom. One game I'd play was *Plan-A-Journey*, described below. The game helps all students to become more familiar with map reading and navigation, and gives non-verbal/ visual learners an opportunity to develop in those areas.

Basic activity

Ask groups to plan a route from Britain to a destination selected at random (drawing a name from a bag, or using dice rolls). Now compile a list of subsidiary places to visit, or items to bring back, or particular things that have to happen on the way. For example, during this journey you must...

- visit three places beginning with B, four places beginning with S, two places beginning with P
- bring back an item appropriate to each country you pass through
- describe one spectacular scene upon your return
- offer a piece of wisdom from someone you met on your travels
- make a list of five ways in which life is different for someone you met at your destination.

And so on.

Extension activities/ variations

- Using a UK or a large-scale regional map, ask small groups of students to set out along a road and, upon coming to a junction, roll the dice to choose which way to go. Ask them to note down the names of places they pass through and speculate on the views they might see from particular vantage points.

- Distribute outline maps of the world (see p.83 & 84), then have groups or individuals colour them in according to their own criteria, or those you lay down at the outset. So maps might be shaded according to:

  - how much a child thinks s/he knows about each country
  - how much a child likes or dislikes countries or people
  - how much countries influence a child's life (TV programmes from the USA, products from different countries, etc.)
  - how developed a child perceives countries to be
  - how keen a child is to visit various places.

The following example is based on the work of one thirteen-year-old girl. Katie used a love-hate scale to illustrate her feelings about various countries she felt she knew something about.

Love
Like
OK
Don't Like
Hate
No knowledge

"I love America because of the TV programmes I watch. I also love Australia because of *Neighbours*. I don't like France because Dad says the Channel Tunnel will allow rabies into Britain. Chinese food is OK but I hate Indian food, because my friend Anabelle says it's too spicy.'

Teachers could use this material to:

- raise cultural or racial differences
- understand more about students' prejudices, stereotypes and generalisations
- give students from other parts of the world, or who have visited places abroad, a chance to input their knowledge and experience
- highlight the ways in which the media represent other peoples and places.

Linked activities

- *Map Maker* (p.80). As children plan their journeys, ask them to suggest possible meanings for the place names they encounter. These can then be compared with actual meanings from reference materials.

- Once students' views about a particular area have been gathered, use *Map Maker* (p.80) to give learners a chance to review their knowledge and/or modify their views.

- Use the *Plan-A-Journey* template after doing the *Chilli Chicken Stir Fry* activity (p.74) to pinpoint where ingredients come from.

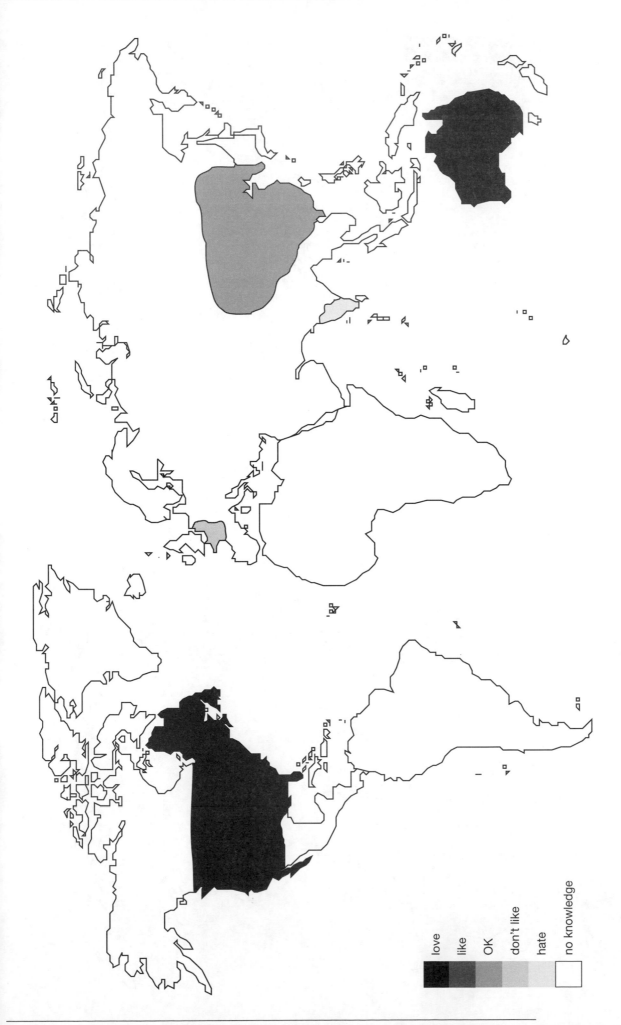

love
like
OK
don't like
hate
no knowledge

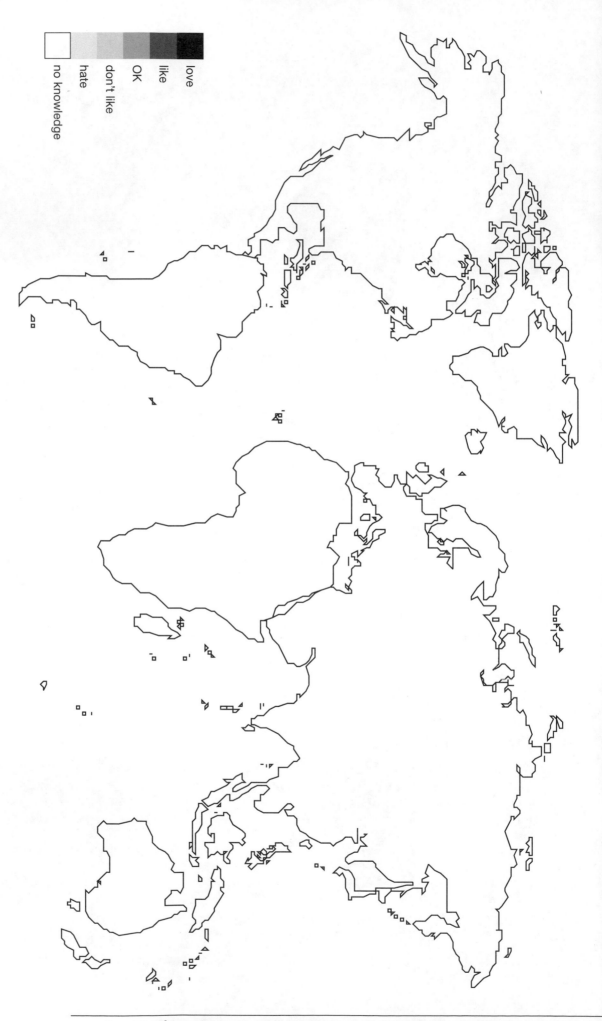

no knowledge

hate

don't like

OK

like

love

> "The 'silly question' is the first intimation of some totally new development"
>
> *Alfred North Whitehead*

Section Four

ASKING QUESTIONS, DECISION MAKING & PROBLEM SOLVING

I think it was Somerset Maugham who said, "There are three golden rules for writing successfully, and nobody knows what they are." I love to quote this whenever I run creative writing / thinking workshops, because it sets the tone immediately and captures the ethos of the work to be done. It is certainly the case that many adults join writing courses so that an 'authority' can 'tell them how to do it.' It does require a certain amount of effort subsequently to point out that a great deal of hard work is needed to drive the creative engine, and that there is really no route map to success – everyone must find their own way forward.

Something that comes close to a 'golden rule' for thinking creatively is to ask questions, and then ask more questions. And I don't mean that as teachers we simply ask questions that allow us to see if children have remembered items of knowledge we've offered up during the lesson. At the very least our questions should test understanding rather than mere recall.

Much more valuable, I feel, is to create an environment where the children feel confident in asking questions. This means ensuring that they are not made to appear ignorant or 'slow' if what they ask is obvious, or if the question seems very oblique to the topic under discussion. Conversely, children ought to be praised, not just for the perspicacity of what they ask, but for the very act of enquiring. The asking of a question reveals the urge to know and to understand. Once that urge has developed in learners, then the meaning-making process jumps to a new level of power, because then it is being consciously and deliberately self-driven.

Many of the activities in this book are geared towards what I have come to call 'Questioneering' – the exploration of knowledge and ideas through creative questioning. Sometimes the questions will be closed and targeted – a request for information. At other times they will be open and exploratory – a search for possibilities, meanings and potentials.

And of course, it is only when information has been gathered in this way that the attendant skills of making decisions and solving problems can be fully developed, so that children can find answers and reach conclusions that are effective for them.

What If?

GROUPING

Whole class

TIME

15 minutes

EQUIPMENT

Counters: about 11

One of the most powerful prompts to creative thinking is the asking of open-ended questions. I say to workshop groups that basically there are two different types of questions: those that have only one answer which is always the same answer (What is the capital of France?), and those that have lots and lots of different answers. Some of those answers will be better than others, but none of them is likely to be 'wrong'. *What If?* is a simple and effective way of demonstrating the point.

Basic activity

Set out an odd number of counters on a table. Explain that you will need four volunteers, forming two teams of two: the rest of the group can then choose to support one or other of the teams. Ask the teams and their supporters to gather at either side of the table. If supporters want to get very involved, they must stand close to the team members; if they want to be less actively involved, they can stand a little further away. This allows all children to become as involved as they feel comfortable with, without leaving anyone out of the game.

Now stand between the two teams and explain that when everyone is ready, you'll ask a *What If?* question. Immediately the two teams will begin having answers. The team to your right may speak at normal volume into your right ear; the team to your left may speak at normal volume into your left ear, simultaneously. Team supporters must not speak to you directly, but can relay their answers by *whispering* them to their team members. For each reasonable answer you receive, that team will get a point in the form of a counter.

When all the counters have been distributed, the game has thirty seconds left to run. During that time, good answers will win points *from the opposing team's store of counters*. After thirty seconds blow a whistle to signal the end of the round. Take care to explain that although one of the teams has accumulated more points than the other, they've all won really because:

a) You've proved to the group that everyone can have lots of ideas if the circumstances are right (and you need to have lots of ideas in order to have good ideas).
b) You now have lots of ideas, and therefore some good ones you can look at in more detail.

NOTE

The important point about this game is that it usually allows all children to become involved. In practice, of course, team supporters don't whisper to their teams – they get terribly excited and yell their answers! (Usually I can hardly hear a thing because of the noise, but nod with enthusiasm as the cascade of spontaneous ideas washes over me.) But don't worry about the din, because it is fleeting and for a good purpose.

The whistle is a useful controlling device. Another way of controlling the group's energy is to run a couple of rounds as I've described, and then tell the class we'll do another one, but in a different way, so they must return to their seats and listen...

Extension activities/ variations

- Ask for two volunteers. One will be the timekeeper, the other will keep a tally of the points. Ask a *What If?* question and wait for the timekeeper to start everyone off. To encourage ideas, suggest that they think under headings such as Transport, Politics, Families, Sport and Entertainment, Housing, Schools, and so on... Explain that when someone has an idea, they put their hand up and wait for you to point to them. Ask them to speak their ideas quickly and clearly: you'll then nod to the score-keeper, who'll notch up the point.

This is a good way to extend the game, for several reasons:
- The children are now sitting at their places, answering by putting up their hands and waiting to be acknowledged, in the conventional way.
- They are working collectively to explore the theme of the question.
- Because they're enthused, involved, and full of energy, they can easily be encouraged to think creatively about 'more serious' topics which can then form the information content of the lesson.
- The next phase of the lesson – writing ideas down, small group discussion, etc., follows on naturally and smoothly from the basis you as the teacher have already set up.

Some What If? questions

What If? questions can be as outrageous and fantastical as you like, because their purpose is to establish a way of thinking and behaving which lends itself to further creative output along more sophisticated lines, and/or carrying greater information content, and/or more specifically aimed at a subject/ area of the curriculum. The game is a springboard and precursor to creative thinking within more advanced structures.

A longer list of open-ended questions can be found elsewhere (*Faction* p.88 and *Parallel World* p.92), but my regular openers are these:

- What if the girls in this group – not the boys, and no other girls – could, whenever they wanted to, become invisible? (Be prepared for lavatorial humour!)

- What if ordinary domestic cats suddenly learned to speak our language and demanded equal rights?

- (Don't ask how this might work...) What if babies were born the size of adults, but people shrank as they grew older, so that senior citizens were no more than one inch tall?

- What if gravity switched off for five minutes every day – but you never knew in advance which five minutes it would be?

It goes without saying that a good creative thinking exercise is to come up with another twenty or thirty equally stimulating *What Ifs?*

Faction

Faction is a term I use to describe any exercise that combines elements of fact and fiction. As a *What If?* variant, *Faction* works by asking questions such as:

- What if all roads became toll roads?
- What if all large mammals except Man became extinct?
- What if a new law was passed in this country limiting parents to one child?
- What if every husband had to have two wives (or vice versa)?
- What if the law changed so that wealth was redistributed evenly and everyone earned the same wage regardless of the job they did?
- What if every child chose exactly what s/he learned at school?
- What if intelligent pocket computers became our voice of conscience?
- What if those computers were linked by radio to a super-mainframe able to pass judgement?

Please Mr Einstein

"Please Mr Einstein, what's it like to go as fast as light...?"

Einstein is well known for his 'thought experiments,' – imaginative scenarios that allowed him to explore phenomena which were not (at that time) amenable to orthodox forms of investigation. Such a thought experiment is a cross between a *What If?* question (p.86) and the activities in the *Point-Of-View and Emotions* section (see p.111). It is an enormously powerful mental tool that, at least initially, frees the experimenter from reliance upon partial and therefore limiting rules and bits of knowledge. It is a kind of self-brainstorming that gives imagination free rein, before the constraints of actuality impose practical boundaries upon what can be done.

Please Mr Einstein endeavours to form a bridge between the uninhibited asking of imaginative questions, and the application of extant knowledge to give shape to the enquiry. The purpose of the exercise is to allow students to assimilate what knowledge they have and to test it through focused investigation.

Basic activity

The game involves asking questions of an imaginary person or other icon. Such a person can be entirely fictitious, such as a character from fantasy or an animal personified, or might be a historical or scientific figure, or famous celebrity. (popular variations...) The point of the activity is not to obtain answers, but to come up with the questions the famous person, etc. might answer if he/she/it were present.

Encourage pertinent questions rather than 'What's your favourite colour' type enquiries. For example:

Please Mr T Rex – How do you manage with such small arms? What happens when you fall down? Do you teach your babies to be as fierce as you are, or are they born that way? Do you ever fight with other meat eating dinosaurs? What was it like back in dinosaur times?

Please Mr Armstrong (Neil Armstrong, first man on the moon) – How did you get to be picked to go first to the moon? How do you move wearing such a bulky spacesuit? What's life like in a cramped rocket ship? How did you decide what to say when you first stepped out on the moon? What did it feel like to be there?

Introduce the person (or whatever) to which you will be addressing questions by way of a brief talk or discussion. Ask students what they would like to know about this person if they were to interview them.

Have students frame their questions in the form of a letter, or simply as a list. Feedback involves sharing the questions as a whole-class activity: if anyone happens to know the answers, that's a bonus!

GROUPING	Individual or small groups initially, then whole class for feedback
TIME	30 minutes
EQUIPMENT	Reference materials

Context Sentences

GROUPING

Whole class or small groups

TIME

15-20 minutes

EQUIPMENT

None

The whole point about *Context Sentences* is that they're out of context! The activity involves asking questions thrown up by such sentences to establish a number of different contexts that allow the sentence to make sense. Context sentences make great starting points for discussion and story making.

Basic activity

Andrews lay slumped across the sofa.

This is a typical context sentence. Ask students what questions they can think of to ask:

- Who is Andrews?
- Is Andrews a man or a woman, or a child?
- Is Andrews dead or asleep or drunk or knocked out?
- Where is Andrews?
- What has happened to cause Andrews to be slumped on the sofa?
- What might happen now?

   And so on.

Context sentences can be oriented towards particular genres, or to evoke certain kinds of questions. You could select suitably thought provoking sentences from existing texts or have students construct their own, then swap.

Another example:

All Jackie saw was the strange glow of its eyes.

- Who is Jackie?
- What is the thing she saw?
- Why do its eyes have a strange glow?
- What kind of glow – an actual glow, a glow of anger, etc.?
- Are they eyes at all? Could Jackie be mistaken?
- Where is Jackie?
- What has brought her to this point?
- What might happen now?

Extension activities/ variations

Perhaps its most immediate use for context sentence work is as a starting point for story making.

To construct narratives, decide at which point in the hypothetical story the context sentence occurs. By continued open questioning about characters, time and place, themes, plot etc., work back to the start, and forwards to possible conclusions.

To clarify the process of using context sentences in a story, I say that creating a story is like hanging washing on a line. To stop the clothes from dragging, you need a number of 'props', which can be cliff-hanger chapter endings, exciting pieces of dialogue, vivid descriptions, etc. A *Context Sentence* exploration can form one high point in a story. What might the others be?

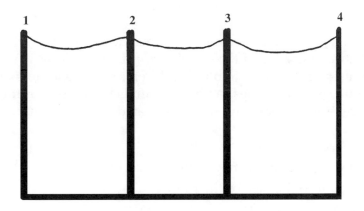

Linked activities

Flesh out the narrative by using devices such as *Circles* (p.47) to explore characters, *Picture Bank* (p.16) to visualise the time and place of the story more clearly, *Theme Cards* (p.17) to focus themes, and *Dice Journey* (p.177) to explore multiple storylines.

Parallel World

This is a much more elaborate version of *What If?* (p.86) and *I Am A Ship* (p.114). The basic premise is that an Earth just like ours exists somewhere – although this other place has one specific difference.

One benefit of using the *Parallel World* idea is that it helps defuse any apprehension children may have in giving the 'wrong' answer when exploring outcomes and consequences. By using, say, the scenario that dinosaurs never became extinct, teachers can introduce concepts of ecology and evolution in such a way that children can 'play' with the facts as their imaginations are engaged by the prospect of T. Rexes and Velociraptors at London Zoo.

Basic activity

Begin by explaining the basic premise, explained above. Decide what the one difference is between Earth and the parallel world – it could be evoked for amusement in order to build children's confidence in using the technique ('In this world females can become invisible whenever they wish'), or to address more serious issues and their associated corpus of knowledge.

Some parallel world differences could be:
- People of your age can shrink at will to one inch tall.
- You can hop into the past or the future.
- You have to trade in your old body for a new one every year.
- You have to share your world with another intelligent, non-human, race.
- The world is ruled by a computer that knows everything.
- Everyone *must* tell the truth for five minutes each day.
- You can see into one other person's mind once each day.
- All people are equal in this world.
- Science doesn't exist.
- Magic exists.

If using *Parallel World* as a brainstorming device, simply encourage children in a class group to throw up as many ideas as they can within, say, a minute. Then encourage them to beat their own score with the next question. Alternatively, there could be a more leisurely discussion on the chosen topic.

Good World / Bad World

Begin with a premise that affects the school, the community, the nation, the world, such as:

- What if the school was awarded a million pounds of Lottery money?
- What if human genetic engineering continued unchecked?
- What if individuals were allowed to do just as they pleased? etc.

Divide the class into two groups (or two sets of smaller groups). Have one group explore the favourable consequences of the premise, and ask the other group to investigate unfavourable outcomes.

Bring the groups together subsequently to contrast shades of opinion.

GROUPING Whole class or small groups

TIME 20-30 minutes

EQUIPMENT None

Knock On

This is a variation on games such as *What If?* (p.86) and *Parallel World* (p.92), where for the purposes of creative thinking it is assumed that one thing has been removed from the world. The technique is not at all frivolous: it can be focused on any subject area to explore the links between objects, people and ideas, by looking at the consequences of a break in the web of interconnectedness.

Knock On **may be used as a stand-alone activity, or as a technique at appropriate points across the curriculum.**

Basic activity

Begin the activity by posing a *Knock On* question such as:

- What would be the knock-on effects of a valuable metal running out?
- What would happen if a link in a food chain were broken?
- What if global pollution meant that long-distance mass transport systems had to be dismantled?
- What if a computer super-virus wiped all hard discs today?

A typical *Knock On* scenario might be:

"What would be the knock-on effects of a valuable metal, say copper, running out...?"

Once the scenario has been given, as a whole class, gather ideas about the purposes of copper in the world. (You may wish to have students research this, which would add to the timespan of the activity.)

To help collect ideas, use headings such as The Home, Industry, Transport, Art, etc. Then use these and other headings to explore the consequences of the scenario. Ideas could be phrased as questions:

- If copper ran out, how could new electrical gadgets be made?
- Would all 'copper' coins be recalled by Government?
- What about copper pipes in our houses? Could we use plastic instead?
- Would bronze (copper and tin) statues be melted down to use old copper?

Extension activities/ variations

You can also use *Knock On* to explore local or personal issues such as:

- What if the police didn't exist and people had to enforce the law themselves?
- What would be the knock-on effect of all cars being banned tomorrow?
- What would be the knock-on effect of money being replaced by bartering?

GROUPING Whole class initially, followed by smaller group work

TIME 20-30 minutes

EQUIPMENT None

- What would be the knock-on effect of video security cameras being installed on every street corner?

- What would be the knock-on effect of supermarkets suddenly vanishing?

Another variation of the game would be to discuss how far students think coincidences are linked.

NOTE   One way of introducing the idea of *Knock On* is to explain the so-called *Butterfly Principle*. This idea, taken from the field of Chaos Theory, says that potentially a butterfly fluttering its wings in China can cause a hurricane in the Gulf of Mexico a couple of weeks later – due to an amplification of air currents stirred up by the insects wings. (The scenario is theoretically possible but hugely unlikely!)

How To Prevent...

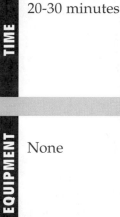

GROUPING Whole class/ groups of about six students

TIME 20-30 minutes

EQUIPMENT None

How to prevent is a way of practising the technique of brainstorming to solve specific problems. As ideas are thrown into the pot, creative connections are made, which could lead to unexpectedly effective solutions.

Practising this problem-solving activity in a fun context can boost students' confidence and enjoyment when it is applied to 'real life' and more serious issues.

Basic activity

Split the class into groups of around six students. Give each group a problem to solve, perhaps from the list below, or from those you have invented. Explain the process of brainstorming, if this has not been done previously (see p.21), emphasising that the aim is to generate and collect ideas, not to criticise or analyse them at this point.

Example problems:

How to prevent:

- cats wailing in the night
- pigeons pooing on statues
- snow building up on your drive or your roof
- sandwiches drying up after a day
- dogs stopping to sniff every lamp post (or worse)
- litter building up in the playground
- condensation forming on windows

Give the groups five to ten minutes to 'storm' the topic, then have them feed back their thoughts to the rest of the class, who may then add to the list of ideas. Assessing the value of the material can follow, as a separate activity.

Voyager

GROUPING

Groups of
4 to 6

TIME

20-30 minutes

EQUIPMENT

Access to
library
resources
(pictures,
music, etc.)

In August-September of 1977 two spacecraft named *Voyager* were launched on an exploratory flight through the Solar System, their speed and trajectories taking them eventually beyond the planets and out into interstellar space.

Although neither probe will reach another star system for tens of thousands of years, it is a significant reflection on the human imagination that both craft carry a package of information about the Earth: its location, nature, inhabitants and their cultures.

The *Voyager* record comprises 118 pictures, greetings in 54 languages, various other sounds ranging from a rocket launch to the song of a humpback whale, and ninety minutes of what is considered to be the world's greatest music.

In short, the two spaceships combine the purposes of a time capsule, a postcard, and a first hello to whoever, or whatever, may happen across them, whenever and wherever that may be...

Basic activity

This activity invites groups of students to consider what *they* would load aboard a similar probe by way of introducing ourselves to the universe: pictures, sounds and other information that must be representative and significant, whether they be grandiose or mundane, personal or universal. How should we portray our planet and its peoples, fairly and honestly?

The story of the *Voyager* probes and their contents can be found in Carl Sagan's comprehensive account *Murmurs From Earth* (see Bibiliography, p.199). A follow-on activity might compare the students' choice with Sagan's.

Board Games

GROUPING

Whole class or small group

TIME

1 hour

EQUIPMENT

Board game templates

Making board games is good fun and creatively stimulating. Ways of using the activity include: thinking of variations on board games that already exist (instead of Snakes and Ladders, try Dragons and Castles, etc); combining areas of study with the creation of a board game (linking, say, spelling lists, items of general knowledge or maths problems with extant or newly devised games); using the board game concept to explore texts (making up a game like Cluedo for an Enid Blyton adventure perhaps?); using board games in conjunction with other *Imagine That...*activities, such as *The Alpha Team* (p.107) or *Abandon Earth* (p.104).

Basic activity

Begin with a preparation lesson, in which students bring in examples of board games and explain how they are played. Common features and principles can be identified, and interesting/ entertaining aspects of different games combined to produce what will hopefully become a collective 'super game':– I like the use of dice and counters; I think the spinner makes it more exciting; I like the way you must go back to the start if you land on a red square; etc. From this collection of features, a number of principles of the game can be devised, and from those, a set of rules can be formulated.

At this point, some thought can be given to the basic layout of the board in terms of areas attached to certain purposes and features of the game. Again, well-known blueprints can be used, singly or in combination, or entirely new layouts might be devised.

Extension activities/ variations

Once the idea of making board games has been introduced, it can be focused and varied.

- Devise board games pertinent to specific subjects or areas of knowledge, or which incorporate facts to be learned or principles to be practised.

- Use novels, films, certain characters, etc., as themes for board games.

- Move out from board-based games to card games.

At its most basic, this simply involves awarding achievement points, certificates, or whatever as children complete each game in a kind of board-game 'assault course'. A more elaborate use of the idea might be to generate a number of games based on, say, the characters and situations in a book, and have groups in the class try out each others' games, each group endeavouring to complete a sequence of them.

Linked activities

Incorporate board games into *Dice Journey* (see p.177) – use the characters, locations and narratives generated in *Dice Journey* as the basis of a game such as a variation on Monopoly, Snap, Ludo, etc. Pull in *Pictures* and *Point-of-View* work as part of the 'play value' of games. Turn chess pieces or draughts pieces into individual characters. Do the same for the counters used in a Snakes and

Ladders variation – and have 'counter characters' working together to help one another through the game, etc.

Board Game Templates

The designs that follow can be used as templates for games, or as separate stages in a single more complex game. Before going further, either preparatory to introducing the idea to the class, or in conjunction with your group, consider the following:

● Brainstorm for initial ideas of the sorts of games the templates could be used for. Add structure to the game, by physically adapting the template (drawing lines, shapes, etc), and/or by beginning to formulate rules.

● Think about the number of players best suited to your selected idea, and how they might move around the board / gain points (dice rolls, spinner, answering questions, chance cards).

● Decide if the interest value of the game could be improved by giving it a physical setting. For instance, could the dots in Dotto represent planets in outer space, stepping-stones across a dangerous river, points on a map, people in a crowd, etc?

● Once these points have been addressed, prepare a first version of the game and play it through. This is the most effective way of seeing if the game is basically viable, and whether 'glitches' exist. Subsequent playings, as the game is refined, will soon lead to the best possible outcome from your initial ideas.

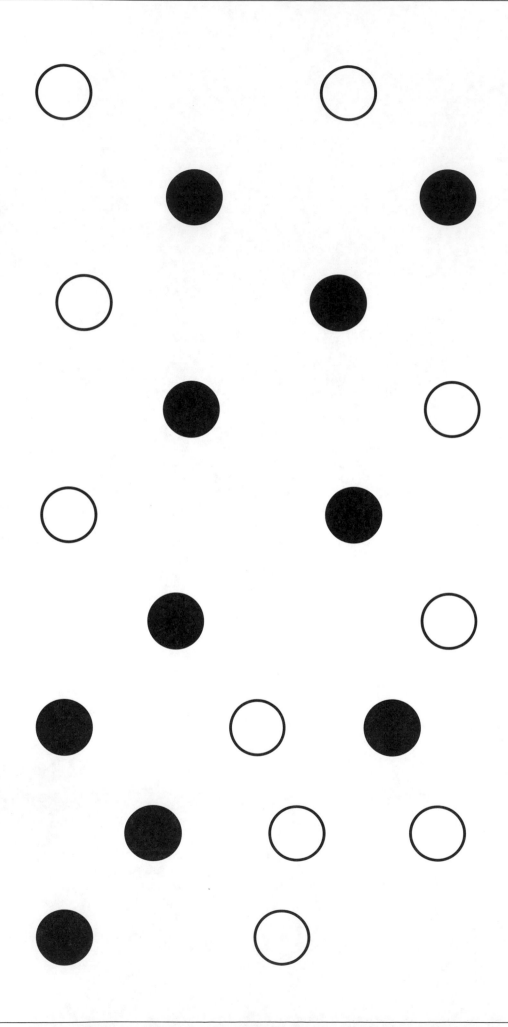

The Why Game

GROUPING

Whole class or pairs

TIME

20 minutes

EQUIPMENT

None

My mother reminds me to this day that I was one of those infuriating children who couldn't stop asking questions, usually following an answer with the dreaded, "But why?" Infuriating, of course, because sometimes adults didn't know why, and needed to fall back on that old reliable response, "Because that's just the way things are..."

The Why Game **isn't so much about finding perfect answers to questions, but exploring possible avenues of enquiry, and also highlighting areas of partial (or no) knowledge. The technique can also be used to generate raw material for story-making activities.**

Basic activity

Begin simply by asking a question that intrigues you, e.g.:- 'Why is the sky blue?' From this point, working in groups perhaps, either make up reasonable-sounding answers, or go and research the topic, always asking "why" after every "because", until no more answers can be found.

E.g.:
  ....Because it's cold up there.
     Why is it cold, up there, when you're so much nearer to the Sun?
     Because the air is thinner, so it doesn't hold as much heat.
     Why is the air thinner?
     Because the Earth's gravity isn't as strong as you go farther away from the surface.
     But why?
     Because gravity is all to do with the amount of stuff that goes to make a planet, or whatever, in space. The more mass you have, the greater the gravity.
     But why?
     Well, because that's the way the universe is made.
     But why?
     Shall we take a break now?

Within the space of a few minutes, the mixture of guesswork, pseudo-science and more-or-less accurate facts certainly provides plenty of opportunity for further research. Or, depending on the topic being explored, the material which has been generated could be used as the basis for a story.

Suitable Topics include:
        Why does the sun rise and set?
        Why don't you get insects the size of elephants?
        Why do we have different languages in the world?
        Why do I get thirsty and need water to drink?
        Why do I have feelings, even if I am only remembering things?
        Why is the moon so far away?

Extension activities/ variations

● A variation of the game is to begin deliberately with an absurd situation, and answer without any regard to factual accuracy...

A man walks into a bank with a banana one day and says, "OK, put up your hands – this is a slip-up!"

Why did he say that?
Because he had a banana in his hand.
Why a banana? It's really silly.
Yes, but this man tended to be lucky even though he was silly. In fact, he believed that the sillier he was, the luckier he became. So he deliberately tried to be as silly as possible. This was the silliest way he could think to rob a bank.
Why didn't the cashiers just laugh at him?
Well, because...

NOTE

Both the questioner and the responder needs to stay on their toes to keep the exchange lively. Also, mutual support is needed to get the most from the game – trying to see how far the ideas will go, rather than trying to catch one another out.

At the very least, playing *The Why Game* is a good laugh; but its deeper purpose is to boost children's confidence in asking questions without fear of ridicule, and to highlight the fact that without asking in the first place, we never find out in the end.

Abandon Earth!

GROUPING

Whole class or groups of up to 6

TIME

30-60 minutes

EQUIPMENT

Board game templates (see p.p.99-101)

Abandon Earth is another popular scenario-as-template game. Apart from the sense of involvement, teamwork and excitement this activity can generate, it also (often implicitly) allows for an exploration of personal values, introduces the concept of prioritisation, and leads to the realisation that things don't happen in isolation – that everything is connected.

Basic activity

Explain to the students that (for whatever reason) the planet is about to become uninhabitable. A number of evacuation programmes are under way, and groups are given the task of planning them – most importantly, of deciding who or what should be taken to safety, and who should be left behind...

The game can be played as simply or as elaborately as you like. It can range from 'Pick ten things to put in your haversack before you board the evacuation ship', to an ongoing debate about who might be worthy of rescuing, together with the construction of long lists of essentials on the journey. Either way, the opportunity exists to draw the distinction between value and cost, and which possessions really are necessary for our survival.

Extension activities/ variations

- *Noah's Ark* – The planet is being flooded and you have been given the task of deciding which living creatures should be accommodated, given that the ark isn't big enough for every species. Draw up your list, and be prepared to justify your reasons...

- *Reprogram* – You have almost created the perfect android. The last stage of the process before the machine can be activated is to program its computer brain with the knowledge, ideas and beliefs you feel it needs. Decide what's worth knowing, and why...

Linked activities

- Combine *Abandon Earth* with a board game template (see *Board Games*, p.97) to create scenarios. Possibilities include collecting a number of essential items as quickly as possible, using a Ludo type layout, or using a Snakes-and-Ladders approach – perhaps count down from 100 to 1; as you make your preparations to leave Earth, you move up the ladder closer to take-off... or slide down a snake when you hit a setback.

- Combine *Abandon Earth* with a *Dice Journey* (p.177) to turn the game into a dramatic storyline.

- Combine *Abandon Earth* with a *How-to-Prevent* brainstorming session (p.95), addressing such issues as: How to prevent rich or powerful people jumping the queue to leave Earth; How to prevent mass panic as disaster approaches; How to prevent Humanity's store of knowledge, art treasures etc. from being damaged or destroyed.

NOTE In 1951, the science fiction film *When Worlds Collide* explored the same theme as *Abandon Earth*. It is a mature and dramatic portrayal of the idea, and has an upbeat ending. The film (available on video) would be a useful resource if using this game with older (10+) children.

Marooned

GROUPING Small groups

TIME 30-60 minutes

EQUIPMENT None

The main aim of this game is to emphasise the idea that we can all be resourceful when the situation arises, and that thinking calmly and creatively allows the most effective access to those resources.

Basic activity

This scenario supposes that you are marooned somewhere – think of some alternatives (in a crippled submarine on the sea bed, in the jungle, in the middle of London with no money, etc.) and roll dice to decide where. The aim of the game is for the group/groups to work out a survival strategy. Students should research accurate information and make a realistic assessment of the dangers, dilemmas and problems to be faced.

Guidance, questions and instructions should be given along with the situation:

- Give an accurate and detailed description of your situation.
- What skills or personal attributes do you (the group) possess that are relevant to the situation?
- What questions do you need to ask before you can proceed?
- Compile a list of useful equipment.
- What decisions do you need to make at this point?
- What do you anticipate you will need to do to survive / escape / succeed?

Results, ideas and conclusions could be presented in a variety of informative and entertaining ways – as short stories, fictional diary entries, letters home, poems, pieces of scripted drama or improvised role play, artwork, etc.

Linked activities

Marooned can be played as a *Dice Journey* (p.177). Once players have been through the basic activity of *Marooned*, use this information as the starting point for a story. Use the *Dice Journey* idea to flesh out character and narrative, and to explore various situations, mishaps and outcomes not thought of initially.

The Alpha Team

GROUPING Small groups

TIME Varied: a 60 minute lesson, or an extended topic lasting several lessons.

EQUIPMENT None

This game allows children to work together, thinking creatively to solve problems and make decisions within the framework of a 'mission' scenario.

Basic activity

Explain to the students that they are a crack team of specialists who are needed from time to time to undertake dangerous missions, sometimes in exotic locations. When presented with a mission (should they choose to accept it) they will need to ask questions and make decisions as they plan and then execute their strategy.

How to proceed:

1. Decide upon the scenario – e.g. a freak electrical storm has disrupted the computer security system at London Zoo, with the result that wild animals have been released into the grounds.

2. Groups are formed either as friendship groups, or to create a deliberate mix of personalities, strengths and weaknesses. With guidance from the teacher, students then decide which particular areas of knowledge and expertise will be required on the mission. Each group member can then choose or be assigned a particular role – Map Reader, Team Leader, Wild Animal Expert, and so on.

NOTE Students can accumulate expertise in particular areas by researching and presenting a small project on any appropriate subject. Colour-coded badges can be made up in recognition of students' knowledge in Biology, Technology, Geography, etc.; or each student can be given a blank badge on which to place coloured sticker-dots as expertise is gained in more subject areas. A variation of this idea is to have students themselves run workshops in various subject areas reflecting their hobbies and interests, and projects they have previously compiled. Subsequently, the different Alpha Teams can be self-selecting (although the tutor will need to ensure that bias and 'peer politics' don't enter into the equation).

3. Decide whether mission members portray themselves in the adventure to come, or generate characters (see *Characters Cards,* p.117 and *Circles,* p.47 for helpful techniques).

4. Teams decide what they need to know and to do to prepare for the mission. For example, suppose the scenario is that many wild animals are loose in London Zoo. The Animal Expert may need to investigate how conservationists safely trap and sedate animals in the wild; the Crowd Controller may need to find a map of the Zoo grounds to plan an evacuation strategy; the Team Leader may need to study news broadcasts to present an appropriate press release of the situation, and so on.

5. The mission begins. The adventure itself can be run as a *Dice Journey* (see p.177) or a discussion, or through drama, and ideally would be a mixture of fun as the narrative unfolds, plus the application of 'real' knowledge to imaginary situations. In short, *The Alpha Team* is a simulation that can be pitched at any level of sophistication or complexity, depending upon time and other resources available.

6. A 'debriefing' session rounds off the activity nicely.

Extension activities/ variations

Interviewing panels could be used to choose Alpha Team members. Have applicants write letters of application stating why they feel *they* should be picked for the job. Interviews may follow, after tutor guidance, on how such procedures should work.

> **TIP**
> You could use the *Genre Chart* on p.158 and your resource banks of pictures, words and theme cards to help generate more ideas for 'missions' – and of course, you can create a new resource bank of missions as they accumulate.

Linked activities

Once a mission has been completed, students can use the material:

- to prepare *Board Games* (p.97) – how to round up the escaped London Zoo animals without being bitten, scratched, stung, trampled...

- to write a *Problem Page* (p.150) letter to another group, to see how they might deal with the situation.

- to make a story out of the mission, perhaps using the *Dice Journey* procedure (p.177).

- to fill out a *Spidergram* (p.46) summarising the main features of the mission.

Magazine Editor

GROUPING — Whole class initially then smaller groups of 4-6

TIME — Several hours, broken down into manageable slots

EQUIPMENT — Examples of magazines

Plenty of schools publish a school magazine, so this activity might be happening where you are anyway. If not, it can be run as a simulation on a smaller scale within a classroom.

Basic activity

Step one is to ask students to bring examples of magazines into school to study (not just read for entertainment!). Analysis will focus on the structure and layout of the magazine, the overall style and the way the items are written: from this you can probably gain an insight into editorial policy.

Next, have groups decide what kind of magazine they want to 'launch'. Make editorial policy explicit. For example, what is the age-range of the magazine and is it intended that younger children should read it anyway (in the same way that teenage magazines are often read by pre-teens); what will be the proportion of stories and other fiction to 'real life' features and articles? What topics should a letters' page or advice column include or avoid? What is the general layout of the publication? Will the publication take a stance on any particular issues?

Issue guidelines to contributors. For example, what sort of material is being sought, and what would not be considered under any circumstances? What length should these be? What styles are acceptable? Can artwork be submitted?

Other guidelines will derive from points of editorial policy once that has been refined. As material accumulates, it will need to be edited (partially rewritten, amended, 'chopped', etc.) to fit page layouts or the 'house style'.

The editorial team can be chosen through negotiation: the teacher may wish to assign specific roles, or students themselves might express a preference for reporting/ interviewing, design and layout, editing text, etc. The number and variety of roles will depend upon how much time and how many resources are available. A useful way of deciding upon 'jobs to do' is to study real magazines, where the roles of the editorial teams are often listed. Information Technology skills could be relevant.

The activity might be long-term, allowing time for closer study of various elements of what goes into a magazine – advertisements (their language and visual impact), small ads/ classifieds, opinion-oriented features as well as the reportage of straight fact. Interviews with real people around the school and in the community might be arranged, together with the coverage of actual topics or events of local interest.

Whatever the timescale, emphasise the importance of deadlines – both for contributors and the editorial team.

TIP
> Involve the whole class in the creation of one magazine of general interest, rather than a number of specialist publications by groups. Or one half of the class could act as contributors, while another half might serve on the editorial team.

Extension activities/ variations

A variation of the activity, *Video / Audio Magazine Editor*, throws up further challenges, joys and nightmares...

> "In the beginner's mind
> there are many possibilities, but
> in the experts mind there are few"
>
> *Shanryu Suzuki*

Section Five

POINTS OF VIEW AND EMOTIONS

One of the most useful and potentially influential concepts to enter the educational arena in recent years is that of 'Emotional Intelligence', which is also the title of the definitive popular book on the subject, written by Daniel Goleman.*

The basis of Goleman's wide-ranging study of emotional capabilities (and lack of them) is that everything we learn has an emotional component. If we accept that learning is the modification of thoughts, feelings and behaviours through experience, then we must also admit that the way we feel about what we learn contributes greatly to the way we understand it – which in turn has implications for the way we are able to use the understandings which are the outcomes of our learning.

Another way of saying this is that experiences and what we learn from them are state-bound or state-specific. That is, powerful associations are formed between experiences, perceptions, understandings and the emotional state we were in at the time. Broadly, this translates into such obvious examples as children doing better at subjects they like, or those taught by teachers they get on with, etc. But the concept cuts deeper than this.

One of Goleman's assertions is that stress inhibits learning. Another is that Emotional Intelligence is a more accurate predictor of future success than IQ (as conventionally defined and measured). These ideas have enormous implications for the emotional landscape within the learning environment, and create an imperative to allow children to be as emotionally resourceful as possible through the use of specific and deliberate strategies for boosting confidence, self-esteem and a sense of wonder and curiosity when learning.

Perhaps the following activities go a little way towards achieving that...

Daniel Goleman, *Emotional Intelligence* (Bloomsbury Paperbacks, 1996)

Positive Self-Image

GROUPING	Individual work
TIME	5-10 minutes
EQUIPMENT	None

People's thoughts shape their view of reality, and in the case of children particularly, those thoughts themselves are absorbed *en bloc* from authority figures such as teachers and parents. The ultimate aim of the activities in this book is to produce open-minded, responsible and independent thinkers with a highly developed sense of fun, and a regard for the ideas and feelings of other people. But that ethos needs to be supported by an equally powerful sense of self-worth; and while many of the games in *Imagine That...* seek to promote confidence and self-esteem, it is sometimes appropriate to make those goals the focus of creative thinking time in the day.

Basic activity

Ask students to sit quietly and make sure they feel comfortable, and explain that the point of the activity is for individuals to reflect on 'what they have going for them'. Everyone can do something well, or has some positive and noteworthy quality.

Tell students to close their eyes or stare at a blank surface, and to think back to the times when they've done something well, or been pleased with an effort they've made. Encourage them to recall favourable comments made by others as a token of pleasure for a job well done, or a kindness shown. Suggest that the effort and the praise feed one another, and that it's easy and desirable to put the emphasis on such things as you go about your day-to-day business.

This is one of the few activities in *Imagine That...* where feedback is not recommended. Students derive the benefits from *Positive-Self Image* through private reflection which is not subject to the pecking order or streetwise cynicism of peer politics. The time is made available, the purpose of the activity is explained, and things are left to take their course.

Some children will get bored and idle the time away; others will remain cynical and treat the activity in a desultory way... But the fact that a proportion of the group waste the opportunity is no argument at all for failing to provide the opportunity in the first place.

My Most _____ Moment

GROUPING — Individual or pair work

TIME — 10-15 minutes basic activity. 30+ minutes for extensions

EQUIPMENT — None

This idea can be used as a wonderful ice-breaker that can quickly allow children (or adults) to overcome the ordeal many people suffer when asked to speak within a group situation. In its most basic form, where children are encouraged to relate events from their own lives, the mix and mood of the group needs to be judged first; and obviously no pressure should be put on children to reveal anything which might make them feel uncomfortable.

Basic activity

Each student (or students if you prefer pair work) is given a card on which is written:

> My most embarrassing moment
>
> My most frightening moment
>
> My most enjoyable moment
>
> My most hilarious moment
>
> And so on.

Invite students to think back to such occasions, and either jot down notes about what they remember, how they felt more specifically, etc.; or working with a partner, to talk about the experience off-the-cuff, including as much or as little detail as individuals feel is appropriate.

Extension activities/ variations

- Have pairs or small groups make up fictitious accounts of most-terrifying, most-embarrassing moments.

- Discuss most _____ moments from another's point-of-view, and/or the point of view of characters from literature, film, the world of politics, etc.

Linked activities

- Link the activity in with story-generation games such as *Dice Journey* (p.177) and *Circles* (p.47), where players are encouraged to explore the range and nuances of emotion characters might feel.

- The idea is also valid when talking about characters from published stories and when extrapolating from pictures (see *Picture Discussion* p.19) – what are the people in the pictures feeling, how would you feel if you were standing in the picture, and so on.

I Am A Ship

GROUPING Whole class

TIME 15-30 minutes

EQUIPMENT Large space

This is a basic visualisation activity. It can be used to introduce a sequence of creative thinking activities, or act as an end-point if an in-depth imagined experience is the aim, perhaps with writing or art as an outcome.

Basic activity

Have children sit or lie comfortably in a suitable space and give them the point-of-view you want them to focus on. This can be specific and narrowly targeted ('You are a kestrel watching its prey... ') or broadly-based and complex ('You are a jungle and everything in it...')

From this point, you as the game leader, can direct attention towards colours, textures, sounds, movement through time or space, etc., and the children simply enjoy the experience as a guided fantasy. Or you can ask for spontaneous responses, again on a group basis, or from individual children if each has been given a different subject to work on.

"You are a ship...Take a minute to gather your thoughts, and imagine what colours you see, what sounds you hear, what you feel like, what's nearby, what's far away..."

John: I am a ship...I'm floating in a calm blue sea.

Gayle: There's nothing around me, just empty water.

Group Leader: What colours do you see?

Gayle: Blue – lots of kinds of blue...

Kathy: And there's green... Streaks of green in the blue sea... And the blue changes, gets deeper, as you look away towards the horizon...

Group Leader: Take a breath and tell me what you smell.

Andrew: Salt and seaweed.

Serena: I smell the rope that's holding my sails in place. It smells of tar... And I smell the fish we've been eating for dinner...

Group Leader: 'We'?

Serena: I'm the crew too. We're scurrying like ants over the decks.

Group Leader: What are you wearing on your feet?

Serena: Kind of, like, slippers. Very light and comfortable.

Group Leader: What sounds do the slippers make on the decks.

Serena: Pitter-pattering -

John: I hear the deck-boards creaking... The whole ship is creaking as it sways -

Angie: My bones are creaking because I'm an old ship. I'm tired of sailing the oceans...

Carl: I'm floating without any cares in the world, letting the tide take me gently wherever it wants to...

NOTE The hoped-for response consists of a vivid and spontaneous mental impression that is active and evolving rather than one which is consciously elaborate and struggled-for: an insight rather than a class exercise.

It is for the group leader to decide how much verbal stimulus to give in the development of the imagined scenarios experienced by the children – but lightness of touch is a good general rule to follow.

Extension activities/ variations

● A variation is to run the activity with the students in pairs or threes. Have them all visualise the same experience and feed ideas through spontaneous talk, or have one student visualising while the other two listen.

● *I Am A Ship* has applications across the curriculum. Use the idea in Science (I am an electron, I am a locust), in Maths (I am a zero, I am a million), in History (I am Sir Walter Raleigh, I am a Roundhead soldier) and so forth.

Who Am I?

GROUPING

Whole class introduction, followed by individual work

TIME

15-20 minutes

EQUIPMENT

None

The purpose of this visualisation is to encourage children to step beyond the obvious assumption that we are the same as the things we possess or the places where we like to be, in an attempt to identify one 'thing' that corresponds to the linguistic convenience of 'I'.

Basic activity

Ask the students to think about the question 'Who am I?' in relation to themselves. Explain that lists are acceptable: I am my body /I am my favourite food / I am my dreams, etc. Gather answers from the students but do not attempt to analyse them.

After five or ten minutes of this, suggest that the things people own do not completely answer the question. Ask about beliefs and values, offering examples – 'I am my belief that we should care for the young and the old/ I am my belief that we all have a part to play in protecting the world,' etc.

Continue perhaps by inviting students to select from or add to their list in written form. Helping them construct an *acrostic poem* (see p.35) consolidates the activity and creates a memento. E.g.:

Sense of humour wherever possible
Tries to get on with everyone
Enthusiastic about hobbies
Values ideas that make me go 'Wow!'
Entertained by day-to-day events

NOTE   *Who Am I?* needs to be used sparingly, since its point is not one that should be laboured. Nor are desired outcomes necessarily immediate. The central question posed by the activity isn't expected to pop up fully formed: rather, it acts as a spur to the imagination and allows insights to build gradually towards a more elegant and less materialistic sense of identity and personal worth.

Linked activities

● *Positive Self Image* (p.112). Have students select and celebrate the empowering aspects of their personalities.

● *Point of View and Emotions* activities (p.111). Ask students to focus on the positive qualities of others.

● *Circles* (p.47). Ask students to draw a circle diagram of themselves (honestly and privately if necessary), and then enlarge the positive circles and shrink the negative ones. Ask them what it would feel like if that change had actually happened. This may sound sophisticated but it is a powerful technique which works well.

Character Cards

GROUPING Individual work/ small groups

TIME 20-30 minutes

EQUIPMENT Magazines to cut up, character templates

At its simplest, *Character Cards* might involve collecting pictures of people cut out of magazines, which can form a resource bank to be used as required.

Alternatively, the activity can take the form of asking students to make up characters, perhaps using the dice-roll technique described below, together with the *Character Profile* or *Character Pyramid* templates overleaf.

Dice-roll character profiling

The first of the templates, as well as several of the suggestions below, use a dice to decide whether the character you are creating possesses certain qualities, and if so at what level. Simply roll the dice to decide whether the quality is there at all – 1-3 = YES; 4-6 = NO. Now roll the dice again to decide how much of that quality the character has: 1 = LOW; 6 = HIGH.

Extension activities/ variations

- Use cut-out pictures of people as a basis for character making. In small groups ask children to offer their impressions: 'I don't like the look of him, I wouldn't trust him at all/ She looks so glamorous, but I bet she's very snobby' ... etc. However stereotypical these ideas are, use them as a basis to develop the characters further through the dice-roll technique.

- Select a character profile that someone else has created, and match it with a picture from the *Picture Bank* (p.16) (being prepared, of course, to justify your decisions).

- Flesh-out dice rolled characters by filling-in a *Character Pyramid* for them.

- Prepare character profiles of famous people; suggest where their various attributes would register on the 1-6 scale.

- Write horoscopes for your card characters.

- Deal out a number of people pictures and/or character profiles. Create a random mix and discuss the circumstances that might have brought them together (as part of an imaginary narrative), and how they might interact from then on.

- Prepare profiles for characters in literature. Introduce a character you have created into the story, and see how that changes the dynamics of the plot.

Template 1: Character Profile

Roll tha dice to fill-in the profile below. 1-3 = Yes, 4-6 = No. There is also a 1-6 scale, where 1 = Low and 6 = High. (See *Dice-roll Character Profiling* on the previous page.)

Having filled in the basic characteristics, use this information to add more details to the profile.

Basic characteristics

Intelligence: _____   Strength: _____

Common Sense: _____   Goodness: _____

Agility: _____   Ambition: _____

Bravery: _____   Attractiveness: _____

(Add others...)

: _____   : _____

: _____   : _____

Other information

Name: _____   Age: _____

Nickname: _____

Catchphrase: _____

Basic Physical Description:

_____

_____

_____

Extra Notes:

_____

_____

_____

_____

Template 2: Character Pyramid

The Pyramid template embodies the idea that we are all 'more than we think we are'. What we see of a person, and our first impressions, amount to the merest glimpse of a much deeper personality. This point could be brought out when the activity is used.

In practical terms, sectioning off the space in which students write about their imagined characters means that they have to choose their words carefully, and perhaps select from a whole raft of ideas they might have about the person they are imagining.

Name / Age

One Unique Detail

Physical Description

Personality

Past
History

Love Is...

GROUPING

Whole class/
small group

TIME

15 minutes

EQUIPMENT

None

We all know the old cliché, 'Love is never having to say you're sorry'. This activity takes the idea further to examine a range of emotions. It can be used in conjunction with several other activities, as suggested below.

Basic activity

Ask students, individually or in groups, to pick an emotion and create as many 'Love Is...' type sayings to define and explain it. Some of those sayings might relate to personal experience, while others will be generally applicable. Use the outcome to explore nuances of emotion, and the links between apparently similar emotions like jealousy and envy.

Example:

> Jealousy is sitting at home while your friends are at the disco.
> Jealousy is wanting and not having.
> Jealousy is sitting in the classroom dreaming of the beach.
> Jealousy is wishing for the past.
> Jealousy is tying knots inside that you can't undo.
> Jealousy is when the sun shines, but not on you.
> Jealousy = envy + anger + regret + bitterness.

Linked activities

● Use the *Love Is...* technique to explore *Emotion Spectrum* (p.132), by picking an emotion and defining it in various ways.

● A *Spidergram* (p.46) could be used after the *Emotion Spectrum* technique, to indicate visually significant links between emotions. A variation is to take an emotion, let's say happiness, and place it in the centre of the template. In nearby boxes write the names of people, places or events associated with happiness – home, school, birthday, my best friend Tony, etc. Use this 'mini mind map' as the basis for the *Love Is...* game:

> Happiness is being home with the TV on a cold, wet winter night.

> Happiness is hearing the school bell at the end of the afternoon.

> Happiness is waking up and remembering it's my birthday.

> Happiness is seeing my best friend Tony when he comes back from holiday.

● Take a *Story Tree* template (p.168) and 'hang' various emotions at the ends of branches. If your explorations of possible narratives take you along a certain branch, incorporate the linked emotion into the story, sharpening up your awareness of that emotion by playing the *Love Is...* game.

'Now' Collage

GROUPING — Whole class

TIME — 1 hour upwards

EQUIPMENT — An assortment of visual materials, glue, scissors, sugar paper

This activity allows learners to represent their ideas about a chosen topic or theme in a visual way. A collage is flexible enough to cater for students who wish to be very structured and realistic in their representations, as well as those who may prefer a much vaguer or more abstract or impressionistic approach.

Basic activity

Ask groups to bring in visual materials that in some way represent the world today – pages of magazines and newspapers, wrappings of shop-bought products, samples of materials, images of celebrities and current fashions and themes, etc. – and have them combine the materials to create a collage that represents vividly the world as it is now. The results can be startling and highly decorative.

Possible topics include:

Youth	Deprivation	Good times
Age	Childhood	Bad times
Poverty	Law	Television
Heroes	Celebration	Environment

Extension activities/ variations

A variation on this activity is to create collages for particular themes, or to target certain films, books and worlds of literature. A Year 9 group I worked with produced a stunning collage based on the dystopian world of George Orwell's *1984*; and I had similarly impressive results with Year 7s who created a collage of John Gordon's book *The Giant Under The Snow.*

Linked activities

● Collage work can often highlight specific points of view – the pessimist, the idealist, the dreamer, the explorer , etc. – and thus is a useful adjunct to other activities such as *Emotion Spectrum* (p.132). Use the *Now Collage* idea to match colours and pictures in order to express certain emotions. Links between emotions and colours go deep into our language.

● A *'Now'* Collage can make a satisfying endpiece to a *Dice Journey* (p.177). Have students create a visual impression of the adventures they've had during their story making.

Double Dare

When I was a little boy, I was in a gang at school called The Double Dare Gang. Every day one of us would dare the others to do something more-or-less mischievous. Of course, the darer was 'double-dared', which meant that *he* had to go through with it as well, or be called a yellow-belly chicken for the rest of the week.

Double Dare takes this idea and uses it to allow learners to explore the boundaries of what is ethically or morally acceptable. It helps children to 'draw the line' and raises their awareness that their actions have consequences for which they are responsible.

Basic activities

One way of using the *Double Dare* activity is to have students think up all kinds of dares for the DD Gang to carry out, then rate them on a scale of 1-10 (for scariness, seriousness, funniness, outrageousness). Discussing or writing about these things is great fun, and can lead to some wonderfully creative stories.

A rather more profound variation uses the double-dare idea to allow individuals to explore their own motivations, ambitions, fears and dreams. Refer to Gregory Stock's excellent *A Book Of Questions* (see Bibliography, p.199) for an adult version of the idea...

- What would you do if you found a wallet containing £1000 on a quiet side street? Would it make a difference if there was a name in the wallet? An address?

- If you could control someone completely for a day, what would you have that person do or say?

- If you could go back to any one point in your life and make one change, what would that change be, and when would you make it?

- How would your eating habits change if you had to find, catch or kill all of your food?

- If you could be someone else for one day, who would it be and what would you do?

- If you could achieve any single ambition, what would it be?

- If you could be an animal for an hour, which animal would you choose and why?

- Would you lie for somebody? If so, think of some situations when you would lie, and why. If you have a particular person in mind, are there any circumstances when you definitely wouldn't lie for that person? Again, why?

- If you could become cleverer by becoming uglier, would you do it? Would you become more attractive by becoming less intelligent?

GROUPING Whole class followed by small group discussion then individual writing

TIME 20-30 minutes

EQUIPMENT None

Journey Through My Body

GROUPING | Whole class

TIME | 30 minutes upwards

EQUIPMENT | Anatomical visuals (pictures, models etc.)

Who could ever forget the sight of Raquel Welch in a white rubber diving suit being pursued by angry blood corpuscles in Richard Fleischer's film *Fantastic Voyage*! It taught me more about the human body than any book ever could (the film, not Raquel Welch in a white rubber diving suit).

For all its wobbly science, the movie highlighted for me the power of visuals and the startling and educational benefits of an altered point-of-view. This activity aims to do the same. It can be combined with modules in Biology, Health Education etc.

Basic activity

It is a good idea to run a preliminary session with anatomical drawings and pictures to help clarify the guided fantasy which follows. The 'guider' then locates the class in a part of the body. It is usually helpful to start on a general/large-scale basis and then zoom in on more specific parts, with questions focusing the pupils' attention: "What sounds can you hear in this place? What colours do you notice?" – but allowing individuals to fill-in details for themselves based upon the visuals they have previously seen.

Once an exploration has been completed – of the whole body, the functioning of an organ, the relationships between elements in a system, or whatever – the insights gained allow biological knowledge to be more accessible and meaningful.

Linked activities

- Use the idea as a *Journeys* visualisation activity (see p.124).
- Use *Journey Through My Body* in conjunction with *Positive Self Image* (p.112) to deliver plenty of 'gee whiz data' to learners about their bodies. Part of feeling good about yourself comes through understanding what an amazing thing your body is.

NOTE

Lennart Nilsson's photographs provide a stunning accompaniment to this activity (see Bibliography, p.199).

Journeys

GROUPING	Whole class
TIME	20 minutes
EQUIPMENT	Maps, resource books

Use *Journeys* as a visualisation device, pure and simple, or link it in with other activities in the book, as suggested below.

Basic activity

Ask students to sit quietly with their eyes closed or stare at a blank space (whichever the students feel comfortable with), and describe one of the journeys below. Teachers will find it helpful to prepare the script beforehand. Note form is fine or other forms you or the children have created. The activity focuses the attention, allows learners to consolidate information they already have about the theme of the journey, and is yet another way of exercising the imagination.

Because we all have preferential learning and thinking styles – some people are principally visual thinkers, others auditory or kinaesthetic – different students will experience their guided/ scripted fantasies in different ways. Inviting students to 'compare notes' afterwards enriches the experience for all.

There are hundreds of journeys to choose from, e.g.:

- The journey of a raindrop through the water cycle, back to being a raindrop.
- The journey of a spider, mouse, moth, etc., through a house or garden.
- The journey of a seed from a dandelion clock.
- The journey of a fallen leaf through a town.
- The journey of a bubblegum card as it is swapped and swapped again.

Compiling a list of such journeys with a group is an enjoyable creative activity in itself of course (and saves a huge amount of effort!).

Linked activities

- After a visualisation, ask learners to invent a symbol or icon to represent what they have experienced – see *Symbols* (p.45).

- Use a parable such as one of the *Day-To-Day Parables* on p.127 as a visualisation. This is, of course, the same as simply listening to a story, the value of which is the non-conscious learning that occurs during the telling.

- Once students are familiar with the routine of 'journeying', have them relate their explorations through a *Story Tree* (p.168). Be sure to tease out descriptions based on all sensory modalities – what was seen, heard, felt, smelt etc.

Memory Temple

GROUPING Small groups followed by whole class discussion

TIME 30 minutes upwards/ 10 minute update slots

EQUIPMENT Paper, pencils

In their book *Cosmic Memory* (see Bibliography, p.199), Sheila Ostrander and Lynn Schroeder talk at length about the incredible feats of memory achieved by noted figures from history, including the astonishing memory palaces of Aristotle, who followed the art of mnemonics supposedly devised by the Greek Ceos.

Mnemonics is a visual memory tool, exploiting the fact that because most of the information we receive arrives in visual form, most people think in images, rather than in abstractions. Furthermore, those images have a greater significance if they can be further linked to the life experience of the individual. This is why force-fed facts that remain unrelated to the life of the student are poorly recalled.

Aristotle's memory temples were vast and complex mental edifices, where areas of knowledge were represented by separate rooms and halls, and where particular facts were to be found in pigeon-holes, niches or drawers, or were embodied in symbols and icons. To access this information, Aristotle went on a self-guided fantasy, striding through the temple's many corridors and levels, until he located the exact site of the knowledge he was seeking.

What Aristotle could do, children can do on a more modest level. Training the memory is practised little enough in schools, and even then often only to get kids through exams by the verbatim regurgitation of information. Meaning-making is lost or forgotten beneath the constant pressure to reproduce facts which embody someone else's opinion of what is useful or valuable to know.

To begin to exploit the mind's natural retentive abilities in a way which students will find to be useful and satisfying, try the following activities:

Basic activity

Working in small groups, one student begins to describe in as much detail as possible the layout of furniture and positions of ornaments, etc., in a room in her house. The other members of the group then collaborate to draw the room and its contents based on the description. When the description has finished, the map is reviewed and amended for accuracy.

The activity can be extended to include an entire house, contents of a scrapbook or photo album, etc.

Extension activities/ variations

● Working the other way round, ask groups to draw rooms they themselves make up, in plan, side view, and so on. Use *Guided Fantasy* techniques (see p.22) to have students visualise cupboards, drawers, books, table-tops, shelves etc. – and encourage them to begin locating facts in these places. You could, for example, get them to invent a personal dictionary, represented by a book that lies on a table, or has its own spot on a particular shelf. There could be twenty-six pages in the book initially, each devoted to a letter of the alphabet. The pages will gradually fill up with words that students wish to remember correctly. If certain words pose a particular problem – such as 'separate' – incorporate little visuals or annotations; for example, *There's **a rat** in separate*. Ask the student to draw a rat by the word in the mental book, so that this fact can be visually, and therefore easily, recalled.

● The process of mnemonics is cumulative. Once groups or individuals have created their modest memory temples, significant objects are not likely to be lost from them. Get students into the habit of regularly adding objects to the 'house' in the form of furniture or decor... They could leave comics lying on a table, each comic telling the story in visual form of a book they've studied, or a story they've heard. A painting might sum-up the characters of a play, and the relationships between them. A mental zoo might display animals in such a way that their country of origin is clear. An ornament, cleverly and carefully devised, might represent a list of words, numbers or other data to be remembered.

Linked activities

● *Dice Journey* (p.177). Investigate a published text by exploring it through a *Dice Journey*. Have different characters from the book located in different rooms in a house, or different locations, Place around those characters objects they are associated with. Have students 'fix' these characters and objects visually in their minds (and/ or using other sensory devices – associated sounds, textures, etc.).

● *Story Tree* (p.168). The *Story Tree* template is itself implicitly a memory device. Colour-code the branches to help learners remember what happened during those parts of the adventure. (Compare this idea with Tony Buzan's mind-mapping techniques described in *Use Your Head*, see Bibliography p.197.)

Day-To-Day Parables

GROUPING Whole class

TIME 10-15 minutes

EQUIPMENT None

On the following pages are three parables, which – yes, I admit it – could be used in assemblies, though their intended purposes are more diverse:

- To deliver important and useful concepts in a simple and palatable way.
- To emphasise the nature and (at least to some extent) the function of symbol and allegory.
- To provide 'templates' for further story making.
- To illustrate that 'lessons of life' are not distant abstractions, but prosaic realities available to everyone.
- To emphasise that there is not necessarily any direct correlation between wisdom and age.
- To allow children to become more self-aware and purposeful in many areas of their life.
- To enhance and underpin in an enjoyable and accessible way the structure of morality and social behaviour expected in any civilised community.

Basic activity

Simply have children listen to the parable/s. Follow the reading with a discussion of the relevant points. (There are some examples of questions to ask after each of the parables).

Linked activities

- Look at *Symbols* (p.45), and discuss with students the symbols that feature within the parables (a path, opposites such as black and white or light and darkness, a ladder, serpents, etc.

- Use *Positive-Self Image* (p.112) before or after a parable, so that children can make creative links between the parables and their own lives. Talk about personal experiences and see if they can be converted into simple parables, thereby emphasising that we all learn from the ordinary circumstances of our lives as much as (or more than) we do from the received wisdom of authority.

The Backwards-Walking Traveller

A little way along the path, a brother and sister saw a most curious sight. Coming towards them was a man, who appeared to be carrying a sack of stones upon his back. He was walking with great determination, almost with anger, and certainly with much grunting and groaning, for the stones were obviously very heavy and a huge burden to him. But stranger still, he was striding backwards, his gaze fixed intently upon the path he had already walked.

After a few moments, the man stopped, bent down, picked up yet another rock and dropped it into his bag, which he then shouldered before carrying on.

"Look out!" yelled the sister, as she spotted the man coming up to a hole in the ground. He seemed not to hear her, and the next second he dropped into the opening with a thud.

He clambered out, muttering and swearing, his anger intensified; grabbed yet another handful of stones and placed them in his sack before resuming his backwards march.

"Excuse me sir," said the brother politely. "But why do you carry that sack of rocks on your shoulders?"

"They remind me of things," he replied promptly. " Look, I'll show you."

Without slowing down, he plucked out a stone and glared at it as he spoke. "This one is rage for all the times people have been unfair to me."

He tossed it back in the sack and snatched another. "And this one is failure... And this, missed opportunities... And this one is youth which has gone forever. It looks small and hardly any weight at all, but I can tell you it's the hardest one of all to bear..."

"Can I ask, sir," said the sister, "why you are walking backwards like this?"

"I can't get the past out of my sight, child," the man told her. " Because all of these stones never cease to remind me of it."

"Doesn't there seem to be an obvious solution to this problem?" the brother said.

The man shrugged. "Why yes. I try not to let it get me down. And whenever I fall into a hole, I jump back up, dust myself off, and start all over again! Now excuse me, I have much to do..."

And the children stared after him as the man paused to pick up another stone, and strode off backwards into the future.

Questions:

- Who do you think the backwards-walking traveller could be?
- Why was he walking backwards?
- What kinds of things might the rocks in his bag remind him of?
- What do you think the ending of the story means?
- Are we like the backwards-walking-traveller in any way?

The Ladybirds

One day Susan was out by herself in the garden. The morning had been wet and thundery, but now the sun was shining warmly down on her as she explored, noticing all kinds of small things for the first time.

After a few minutes of wandering thus, she came across two ladybirds on a leaf. They were engaged in what looked to be a fierce struggle, locked together in combat as they rolled this way and that. Both ladybirds were startlingly different from anything Susan had seen before. One was pure white, yet had a single black spot in the middle of its back. The other was pure black, and in the centre of *its* back was a solitary white dot.

Susan liked the look of the white ladybird: it seemed clean and nice, and kind of sunny like the afternoon had turned out. On the other hand, the appearance of the black ladybird frightened her rather: it looked sinister, menacing and evil.

The child watched as a subtle balance tipped and the black ladybird rolled on top of its white opponent. Then, after some seconds of effort, the tables were turned and the white ladybird managed to gain the advantage. But then the black enemy, with a renewed effort, regained its ascendancy...

Susan decided she had better do something about this, before the white ladybird was harmed or killed.

She reached out to separate the two insects, but found they could not be moved. No matter how hard she tried, she was unable to draw the ladybirds apart, so closely and tightly were they intertwined.

She became so engrossed in her mission that for some minutes she failed to notice the black clouds piling up in the sky, until a rumble of thunder alerted her.

Susan gazed up, apprehensive at first, then relieved to see that the storm was coming to nothing, the clouds sliding away to let the sun once more shine brilliantly down.

And then, understanding, she let the ladybirds go, because the force that bound them was no different to that which made the day and the night, summer and winter, life and death, the stars and the spaces between them.

Questions:

- Do the ladybirds fighting together remind you of anything?
- How are 'black' and 'white' linked with the idea of fighting?
- Why do you think Susan wasn't able to move the ladybirds?
- What was it that Susan understood at the end of the story?

Ladders And Snakes

Susan and Jonathan were walking through the outskirts of Appletree Town one day when they came upon a most unusual sight.

There ahead of them stood a huge stone tower that they had not noticed before. It reached up and up towards heaven – though it could hardly be expected to get there, they thought, since heaven was an infinity away in that direction.

But there was something else hindering the many grown-ups who appeared to be the builders of this mighty structure. Although they were yelling and shouting at one another at the tops of their voices, it seemed they were all speaking in different languages, and so nobody could understand what anybody else happened to be saying. The result of this was that while half of the grown-ups were busy piling stone on stone, the other half were equally intent on removing them and placing them elsewhere. Thus, the tower grew at a rate of two steps forward and one step back.

The builders reached the higher galleries of the tower by means of long flimsy ladders. Many of them looked dangerously balanced; and sometimes one person would deliberately push another off his perch. When this happened, the victim would cling precariously to any ledge or crevice he could find, scramble up, and then attempt to do unto others as he had been done to.

The children thought this very odd indeed.

Then Susan happened to crane her neck to look upwards, and right at the top of the tower she caught sight of the serpent. It was weaving and writhing amongst the topmost stones, flickering its tongue towards the people who were climbing closest.

She pointed this snake out to her companion.

"Huh, it doesn't look so scary from here, "Jonathan commented... But it would look bigger and scarier the closer you got, he thought to himself with a shiver.

Suddenly, and without warning, a man came tumbling off his ladder. He spun through the air and came crashing to the ground with a thud.

"I don't think you realised the gravity of the situation," Jonathan told him as the man stood up and brushed himself off.

He looked at the children with their bright smiles and open faces, and beamed at them.

"No, I didn't," he admitted. "But I think from now on I'll take myself more *lightly*."

Questions:

- Why were some grown-ups building the tower while others were taking it down?
- In what ways could Susan and Jonathan be said to be wiser than the adults?
- What happens in Ladder And Snakes that couldn't actually happen?
- In what sense, though, is the story very much like real life?
- Can you think of more examples of grown-ups squabbling like the ones in the story?
- Who or what do you think the serpent is in the story?
- What does it mean to 'take yourself lightly'?

Age Gap

GROUPING Whole class, followed by small group work

TIME 30 minutes

EQUIPMENT None

This is one variation of a more general thinking skill I call *Lensing* (see p.134). It is an awareness-heightening game, the purpose of which is to appreciate how people of different ages look at the world and themselves.

Basic activity

Begin the activity by chatting around the theme: what does it feel like to be a certain age? How does the group's point of view differ from those of older/ younger people? Can students remember what it was like to be younger? What problems or difficulties arise between people of different ages?

Follow this discussion by suggesting that the class can now design a new shopping mall, bearing in mind the needs of elderly people.

- Talk first about any shopping malls the children already know.
- Ask if there are any aspects of the design which have taken older people into account, or which obviously *haven't* done so.
- Gather ideas about improving the mall's layout with emphasis on access for older people.
- Embody the ideas in drawings or written descriptions of the new, user-friendly shopping area.

Extension activities/ variations

Follow on with activities such as:

- Writing a story for younger children.
- Preparing a talk or presentation on a chosen topic for an audience of a certain age.
- Inviting groups to introduce a topic they consider to be specific to their own age-group – pop music, comics, toys, particular fashions – to a different age-group.

NOTE The aim of these activities should be to inform and entertain, rather than defend or entrench!

A Day In The Life

A further variation of the point-of-view idea is to ask students to create a presentation of a day in the life of another person, a creature, an object, or whatever. (The term 'day' can be used metaphorically to include any appropriate time-span.)

Once groups have chosen their subject, they should be encouraged to undertake a little research to gather facts – though the outcome need not of course be scientifically accurate. The outcome might be a poem, a piece of dance/drama, a collage, a story, a flow diagram – or any or all of these.

Emotion Spectrum

GROUPING

Whole class

TIME

20 minutes

EQUIPMENT

None

This is a technique designed to raise children's awareness of the range and variety of human emotions. Its most immediate application is in discussing characters during story making, or when looking at published texts. However, its wider use comes by inviting students to 'look inside' and explore creatively the nature of emotion, becoming more sensitive to their own, and therefore to other people's, feelings.

Basic activity

Begin using *Emotion Spectrum* by looking with students at individual emotions themselves. Encourage discussion of the meaning of the word: what the *emotion* feels like; under what circumstances might it arise...? Personal anecdote might be appropriate here, but needs to be very sensitively handled.

Follow this by using the *Emotion Spectrum* chart (p.133) to explore a range of emotions according to intensity and frequency. The chart is intended to relate emotions according to their frequency in one's life, and how negatively or positively powerful they are/were. Thus, boredom might be ongoing in someone's life, but be part of the 'emotional background', manifesting at a low level. On the other hand, awe which is an extreme emotion, and a highly positive one, might be experienced only rarely.

Extension activities/ variations

- Ask students to find extracts from stories or pictures from comics that illustrate different emotions.

- Have students describe situations – either hypothetical events, or ones they have actually experienced – and discuss the emotions one might feel at such times.

- Look at the expression of emotions in art, literature, music, the media. Put names to the emotions represented.

Linked activities

Combine *Emotion Spectrum* with:

- the *Circles* template (p.47) to help you explore where and how emotions might overlap.

E.g.

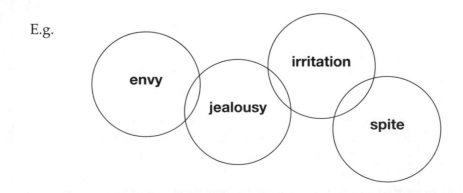

- *What If?* (p.86). Rather than just having ideas about what might happen in a *What If?* scenario, look at how people might feel about it too.

- *Story Tree* (p.168). Hang emotions on the ends of branches, so that students take these into account as they explore narrative possibilities.

Example Emotion Spectrum

10		ecstasy		bliss
9	love	serenity	awe	
8	satisfaction	delight		contentment
7			wonderment	
+ 6	happiness			
5	joy	passion	exhilaration	
4	gladness	nostalgia	pride	
3		compasssion		
2	excitement	relief		
1	anticipation			
——— 0	boredom	apathy		———
1		irritation		
2	embarrassment		nervousness	
3	sadness	chagrin		
4	regret	sorrow	dejection	
— 5	envy	fear	loneliness	
6	jealousy	rage		
7			fury	
8		misery	horror	
9			grief	
10			desolation	terror
			despair	
	everyday common uncommon rare very rare			

Degree / Frequency ⟶

Lensing

GROUPING

Whole class

TIME

20-30 minutes

EQUIPMENT

None

Basically, *Lensing* is the process of consciously and deliberately looking at something in a different way. One way of having new ideas is to see how broad themes or plots used in one genre (style of story) work out in another. So we might take the idea of a soulless but powerful computer – a Science Fiction motif – and 'lens' it through the Fantasy genre, to see how the idea would fit in a fantasy story.

Basic activity

Present the group with the interlinked circles of the three genres (see below), pointing out that useful storylines and situations can be found by looking at the overlap areas – the areas where Horror blends into Fantasy, and where Fantasy begins to change into Science Fiction. Spend time discussing the books and films that exist in these areas to highlight the point that a fresh approach to an existing idea is often an effective substitute for originality.

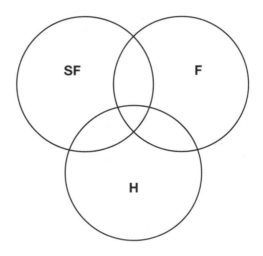

The next stage is to step into the 'main territory' of, say, the world of Science Fiction, and lens chosen SF concepts in different ways. For example, take the idea of alien invasion. It could translate into a fantasy format as an invasion of pixies into the town because their woodland has been destroyed by a new road development. Or an infestation of dragons in an ordinary suburban street. Or a wizards' convention held in a local village hall. The same concept lensed through the horror genre immediately produces all kinds of rampaging monsters!

As another example, consider the theme of 'the threat of modern technology'. I used this idea in my novel *Panic Station*, but lensed it through the horror genre. The plot revolved around the ghost of a failed movie director who returned to wreak revenge and force people to watch his dreadful films. He did this by haunting a new cable TV station in a town, causing the cables to grow through the ground like roots, and plug themselves into people's televisions. Once folks started to watch the new channel, they fell under its influence and could not break free. How does the story resolve, do you think?

Extension activities/ variations

The application for genre work in an English syllabus is clear. But Lensing, and the related concept of overlap areas, can be used in many different ways...

- Take a theme or project – perhaps a Book Week – and....
  1. Draw a circle to represent the aims and objectives of the Book Week.
  2. Draw overlapping circles to represent various, usually unrelated, educational goals. Try lensing mathematical ability with self-esteem, spelling accuracy with inventing a character for a story, organisational skills with a day-to-day parable, curriculum development with a story tree...
  3. Draw circles to represent different subject areas.
  4. Look at the overlap areas and work out what they would contain.
  5. Lens the Book Week concept through a subject area such as Biology or Personal & Social Education.

What other new ideas and directions come to mind?

Significance

This is a discussion activity used best with students who are already familiar with the kinds of thinking and the attitudes advocated in this book. Its main aim is to highlight how easily we can make assumptions and use stereotyping in our judgements of people and events. How far can we truly know a book by looking at its cover?

Basic activity

1. Ask students to bring in a variety of items and/or use the *Sundries Bag* (p.17). Accumulate video clips, pictures, descriptions of people, places, events, bits of junk and bric-a-brac.

2. As a class or in smaller groups, describe each item or picture, noticing details in all sensory modalities. At this stage, withhold ideas about what such details suggest.

3. Ask students to pretend that every item being discussed has some great significance or importance, at least for somebody. Brainstorm what the various details could mean. It doesn't matter if such judgements are 'right' or accurate, or not. The example below illustrates the point.

"That boy has frayed jeans with no pockets."

"That's because he's an eccentric millionaire who doesn't want people to think he's showing off about his money."

"His father is the director of a clothing company. He's trying to create a new fashion in hippie-type clothes, and the boy is helping to publicise some new designs."

"All his life this kid has done what he's told – but now, on his fifteenth birthday – he's decided he isn't going to be pushed around any more. Wearing these 'unacceptable' jeans is his way of starting to kick back."

And so on.

Free discussion around these little focal points will quickly reveal patterns of thinking in the students themselves: the one who always jumps to the most outrageous explanation, the one who tends to look on the dark side, or who stereotypes, or who takes naive views, or who is unfailingly critical...

These are observations which the creative teacher can use to enhance learning (rather than as points of behaviour to judge or to criticise).

Significance can be run as a stand-alone, awareness-raising activity, although the principles have applications across the curriculum, whenever the teacher wishes to address snap judgements, generalisations, or 'automatic thinking' in the students.

Extension activities/ variations

An elaboration of the game which works better perhaps with older students is to prime certain members of the group to display particular patterns of thinking deliberately – such as taking the pessimistic view, being naively idealistic, being sexist, ageist (or any other 'ist') when discussing other people, or issues raised in the course of study. This fuels discussion and debate, and makes the others more aware that a habit of thought based on an unchallenged viewpoint is like a blunted tool in a box filled with many fine instruments, lying unused.

GROUPING

Whole class or small groups

TIME

20-30 minutes

EQUIPMENT

Assorted items or *Sundries Bag* (see p.17)

Apathy

GROUPING Whole class

TIME 15-20 minutes

EQUIPMENT News clippings/ video clips

As teachers we all encounter what I call the 'Don't know and don't care' syndrome. Sometimes, on those bad days, apathy lies like the heavy sediment at the bottom of the learning pond. But it seems to me that the best way to deal with it is to look at it to find out how it works.

Basic activity

Begin by asking students to express their level of interest in a range of ideas or circumstances. Use newspaper headlines, video clips, snippets of literature, pictures; and have students register how interested (or otherwise) they are in these things. Invoke a 1-6 scale if you wish, and give it a survey-type format.

Continue by exploring the reasons *why* these items are interesting or dull. This approaches the heart of the problem because students will then be revealing things about themselves, however implicitly. Consider how dull items can be made interesting. How would the students themselves present these items if their job was to make them more stimulating to others? In other words, examine the mechanics of interest with a view to exploiting that knowledge in future presentations.

> **TIP**
>
> At worst, *Apathy* can sink into a general gripe about school, home, the state of the nation and the future of the world. As group leader, you should work to prevent this happening. Focus the activity upon an analysis of 'the interest factor' rather than an expression of general dissatisfaction.
>
> One aspect of flawed (i.e. uncreative) thinking is to see things in black or white. If this tendency is not addressed, it becomes a habit of thinking which leads to automatic reactions and views based upon ignorance, which are not updated in the light of new information.

Wide World

GROUPING

Whole class

TIME

15 minutes

EQUIPMENT

None

Wide World does for the planet what *Journey Through My Body* (p.123) does for one's physical self-awareness. The aim of the activity is to allow students to gain and then reinforce a sense of perspective of themselves in the world; a sense that we are all in the same boat and can each of us do something to help keep it afloat.

Basic activity

Ask the class to sit quietly and make sure that they are comfortable, then hold up a picture of the Earth in space. Basic facts about the planet can be given, then the guided fantasy begins. Students close their eyes or stare at a blank surface or the Earth image, as the visualisation takes them over the icy wastes of the Poles, across oceans, over mountains, through jungles, into volcanoes, etc.

Visualisations can end in a number of ways. The group leader can home-in on the country, county, neighbourhood, street, building and room where the exercise is taking place, thus bringing participants 'back to themselves'; or zoom out to an image of the whole Earth once again.

A suggested script follows, but the real value is in writing *Wide World* scripts for more specific purposes such as:

- Incorporating geographical/ ecological information as part of a course of study.

- Focusing in on differences between our climate/ culture and another.

- Highlighting the plight of an endangered species.

- Sharpening learners' ability to describe details using all sensory modalities.

- Exploring different viewpoints and perspectives in description.

Linked activities

- Link the activity with *Theme Cards* (p.17). Creating separate cards to highlight themes for *Wide World* visualisations you want to explore – such as climate, extinction, pollution, deserts, the sea, etc. – helps focus subsequent work.

- Ask students to write 'mini visualisations' to develop a resource bank. A descriptive paragraph can then be used as a basis for more extended writing.

Wide World Visualisation

> **NOTE**
>
> Read slowly, with plenty of pauses... to allow children to assimilate each impression. The visualisation is in 'chunks': feel free to add chunks to change, amend, enrich the journey.

...With the Earth in front of you now, floating in space... drift slowly over the top of the planet... until you are looking down at the pole... White... jagged... icy... surrounded by dark ocean... Let yourself sink a little closer... until you can see mountains of ice... great deserts of snow and crystal... huge icebergs motionless in the sea... pale mist swirls around...

...Choose a direction and float that way... picking up speed... until the land begins to change around you... snow and ice give way to trees... endless forests of pine and spruce... You fly through rain... And there's the boom of thunder... and quick flickers of lightning in the stormy sky...

...Lift up above it... Sail through a sunny blue sky... over the clouds and storms... Until they clear beneath you... Thousands of feet below... You see craggy mountains... Deep jungle valleys... cascading waterfalls... swirling rivers... great lakes coloured many shadows of green and blue...

...Drift towards them now... swooping low... Feel the cool air rush past your face... The land speeds by... You hear animals calling in the distance... And flocks of birds sweep like leaves ahead of you, then below and behind, moving out of sight...

...Ahead, there's the sea once more... crumbling cliffs... a beach... miles of sand dunes... Zoom across, faster than any plane... Come at last to more familiar sights... Woodlands... countryside... hills and valleys... fields...

...You're nearing home now... places you know... a village... a landmark... Notice the weather... the colour of the sky... warm or cool... sunny or dull... Soar higher to see the whole area spread out below you... Then drift down slowly... noticing buildings... gardens... people and traffic in the streets...

...Notice this building now... getting closer... You can drift through the roof like a ghost... Drift closer... closer... Notice the sounds around you, the aromas in the air... Realise that you are back inside your body... Your journey is at an end... Think back to where you've been, then stretch and come back fully to yourself...

> "Catch the vigorous horse
> of your mind"
>
> *Zen Saying*

Section Six

CONFIDENCE AND SOCIALISATION

*T*his is, of course, a huge area and one of fundamental importance in the field of effective learning. If I may, I'd like to tell you two brief stories which brought home to me how absolutely vital *interpersonal* and *intrapersonal* skills are in the education of any child...

The first experience happened to me when I was studying A Level English. The study group was fairly small, about eight of us, and our teacher, Mr Robertson, was a very intense and rather serious man, deeply dedicated to his subject. The format of most of our sessions was to read a poem or extract and then 'discuss' it. Such discussions usually meant our teacher talking at great length, mainly because none of us dared to voice our opinions. One time, we read a poem by Thomas Hardy called *The Garden Seat*, after which Mr Robertson asked for our view. A long, awkward and familiar silence ensued until one of us dared to speak up. " Well I thought it was a terrible poem. It was trite, unoriginal, maudlin and obvious..." The silence deepened after that, and we expected swift and severe punishment. Instead, Mr Robertson smiled and opened his hands to include us all. "Ladies and gentlemen," he beamed. " Your English Literature course has now begun!"

Years later I took part in an Activities Week at the school where I worked. The normal timetable was abandoned, and children spent the time on other projects. I offered to be 'the adult presence' for a fantasy role-play week, where children came and ran various war-games such as 'Dungeons & Dragons'. One of the groups was under the control of a very quiet boy whom I recognised as a Set Four (bottom group) pupil in English. I was puzzled, then intrigued, to watch this lad take firm and efficient command of the group, directing Year Eight and Nine pupils very effectively and with great confidence. On the second day, I went over and asked, "How come Mark is the boss here?" "Sir," said one of the big Year Nines. "Because he knows everything about the game." I asked what that meant. The Year Nine boy promptly dragged a bulky 'battle manual' out of his holdall. It was filled with detailed instructions, directions, campaign scenarios, facts and figures. Mark had memorised it.

Needless to say, perhaps, I am still working on the implications and benefits of these two experiences...

Peas In A Pod

GROUPING
Whole class or
small group

TIME
15-20 minutes

EQUIPMENT
None

This game can be run as smaller group work in a classroom, or with class-sized groups if a large open space is available. The game stimulates 'on the run' creative thinking and improvisation, and there's also an important visualisation component. *Peas In A Pod* is a quick and easy way for children to develop confidence through involvement and fun.

Basic activity

Ask the children to space themselves out around the room. Explain that you are going to call out a list of items (such as the one below) and that the aim of the game is for the children to form clusters representing those items as quickly as possible – then freeze. Now call out each item in turn.

- Four peas in a pod
- Six links in a chain
- Two walnut-halves in a shell
- Ten ants in a nest
- Eight pages in a book
- Twelve stars in a constellation
- Nine planets orbiting the sun
- Five balloons in a bunch
- Three fishing boats bobbing in the sea
- Thirty (or whole group) leaves blowing in the wind
- Ten bees in a hive
- Eleven chips wrapped in newspaper
- Seven tools in a toolbox (each tool must be different).

New lists can be devised which are pertinent to a particular theme or topic.

Linked activities

- Once you have run *Peas In A Pod*, have students re-form into chosen groupings and have a *Point Of View and Emotions* session (see Section Five), asking questions which allow them to experience the world from the viewpoint of the items they have just been representing. For example, *Three fishing boats bobbing on the sea* – what does it feel like to move in this way in the water? What colours do you see in the ocean? Look up, what's in the sky? Describe it. What does the sea smell like? Describe the texture of the wood in the fishing boat.

Go on to run a *Guided Fantasy* (p.22). This is a natural extension of the *Point Of View and Emotions* work; it is more elaborate and detailed. Once learners have been 'three fishing boats in the sea', enrich the visualisation subsequently. Have children imagine the daily life of the people who take those boats out to fish; conjure up a storm and ask students to feed back what is happening; have the boats discover a strange new island, and let the children explore it and tell you what's there...

Artist And Instructor

GROUPING | Whole class

TIME | 20-30 minutes

EQUIPMENT | None

This game always proves to be a popular filler, and could be put to use also as a way of practising vocabulary.

Basic activity

Pick two students from the group, one to be the 'artist', the other taking the role of 'instructor'. The artist positions herself by the board or OHP with chalk or marker-pen poised, ready to receive instructions.

Meanwhile, the group leader writes down the name of an object which can be drawn without too much difficulty – a helicopter, a giraffe, a pineapple, etc. – and shows this to the instructor, whose job it is to guide the artist in drawing the object without telling her what it is. In fact, the instructor can only refer to the object in terms of the basic shapes of which it is composed. No one else in the class knows what the object is; it is their job to guess, putting up hands and waiting to be asked. If working with a small group, you can allow players to call out their guesses. This adds to the excitement, but gets noisy in a whole-class setting!

As an example, here's how the instructor might begin to guide the artist into drawing the cat below...

"Draw a large circle in the middle of the board. Now draw a smaller circle on top of the larger one – the smaller circle should be about a third of the size of the larger one. OK, now on top of the smaller circle and at about the eleven o'clock position... What, you don't understand that? OK, I mean a little bit to the left side of the very top of the smaller circle – draw a tall thin triangular shape... No, that's too tall and thin. Rub it out and do it again... That's better. Now draw a similar shape to the right of the top of the smaller circle...

"Now I want you to put a small dot in the very centre of the smaller circle. To the left of that dot and a little above it, draw a small circle – too big, make it smaller... Now do a similar circle to the upper right of the dot. Now below the dot-and-two-circles, but still within the smaller circle – yes, the smaller circle on top of the big circle – I want you to draw a crescent shape... I don't want it to go right to the inner edges of the smaller circle..."

Of course, some members of the class will have guessed the object long before the drawing is complete. Judge the difficulty of objects according to the abilities of the group; and add to the exercise by asking instructors to use particular words, like *crescent, converging,* and so on.

Notes And Excuses

GROUPING

Individual
writing

TIME

20-30 minutes

EQUIPMENT

None

This idea arose after a discussion I had with a group of Year Nines about suspension of disbelief. The aim of the game is to have students think of an excuse and/or write a note explaining why they are late to school.

This is a good filler game, but it can also be used as the basis for examining: exaggeration in the media; sensationalist claims ("I was abducted by alien octopuses"); folklore, legend and myth; the use of emotive language; thinking techniques (see books like de Bono's *Lateral Thinking*, Robert Thouless's classic *Straight And Crooked Thinking*, etc., listed in the Bibliography on p.197).

Basic activity

Allow the students 10-15 minutes to write their notes explaining why they are late to school. There are a number of variations:

1. Make the excuses as outrageous / bizarre / unbelievable as possible.
2. Make them thoroughly believable.
3. Make them reasonable to begin with, but increasingly exaggerated and debatable. For example:

Dear Mr Bowkett,

　I am sorry my son Wayne missed your lesson the other day, but he has been ill recently and needed to visit the doctor. On Monday, the day of your lesson, I sent Wayne to see Dr Talbot at the medical centre. He needed to have his hands examined, because there were some strange hairs growing out of his palms. Dr Talbot said he was sorry, but the hairs meant Wayne was a werewolf. Wayne has never been a shy boy, Mr Bowkett, as you know, and asked the doctor how he knew this. Whereupon, Dr Talbot himself sprouted hair all over, and huge fangs, and turned into a werewolf too.

　I am also letting you know that Wayne hasn't done his homework either, as his claws make it difficult for him to write.

Your sincerely,
Eleanor, P. Garou.

Now ask each student in turn to read out his/her excuse.

A number of students could form a panel to judge the merits of the notes and excuses presented, according to the criteria decided upon – the simplest notes or most elaborate, those using the longest and most posh-sounding words, the ones containing the cleverest language, the ones which are most complimentary to the recipient...

Safe Haven

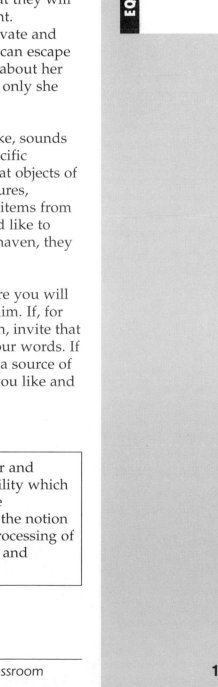

GROUPING — Individual work

TIME — 15 minutes

EQUIPMENT — None

This is an ancient and powerful technique that makes use of the principle that repeating a visualisation brings positive, cumulative effects. *Safe Haven* can be used in many contexts: as a basic relaxation device, as a means of allowing reflection to occur, problems to be examined, decisions to be made, dilemmas to be resolved, etc.

The basic purpose of *Safe Haven* in this context is to find out things you didn't know you knew! We all have an inner wisdom, which we can use to help us cope with our everyday lives. Hunches, feelings, anticipations, ideas out-of-the-blue – all constitute information coming up from the subconscious part of the mind. *Safe Haven* is a device for gaining access to that inner knowledge and wisdom.

Basic activity

Have students close their eyes or stare at a blank surface. Explain that they will soon be asked to imagine a place that's safe, comfortable and pleasant. Emphasise that each of them will create a place that's individual, private and where they will never be disturbed – a personal place to which they can escape and where they can think. No student will be asked to say anything about her safe haven unless she wants to: it is entirely her own domain, where only she goes unless she deliberately invites anyone to share the experience.

Ask students to focus their attention on what the safe haven looks like, sounds and smells like, feels like... etc. (see *Ten Questions*, p.53, for more specific guidance). Have each student explore it thoroughly. Then suggest that objects of personal significance and value can be placed there: ornaments, pictures, jewellery, and so on. These objects can represent real possessions, or items from the past that may no longer exist, or things that the individual would like to own. But in any case, once those items have been placed in the safe haven, they are secure and can be looked at whenever you choose.

Point out also that because this is a *safe* haven, whenever you go there you will feel relaxed, secure and confident in your ability to achieve a given aim. If, for instance, you want to say something of importance to another person, invite that person into your safe haven to test his or her possible reactions to your words. If you are having a problem of some kind, go to the safe haven to find a source of ideas, advice or inspiration – a book of wisdom, perhaps; a teacher you like and trust; an informative picture or video...

NOTE

The power to imagine – to concentrate, visualise, remember and anticipate creatively – exercised in this activity is a natural ability which enhances the more conventionally acceptable mental skills of the intellectual part of the mind. Every group leader should consider the notion that content-based lessons, which focus only on the intellectual processing of facts, embody a small and limited definition of what Education is and should be about.

Superhero

GROUPING
Whole class intially, then smaller groups

TIME
Flexible time span

EQUIPMENT
Pictures of super heroes/ villains

Inventing a new superhero or superheroine is great fun, and there are also many educational benefits. Today's superpeople are the direct descendants of folk heroes and, farther back, of the icons of classical mythology. Superheroes embody high ideals, noble aims and selfless actions: a huge amount of work can be drawn together by this device in the areas of morals and ethics, personal conduct and the nature of concepts such as community and altruism. Designing a superhero isn't just drawing colourful costumes to while away a dreary Friday afternoon...

Basic activity

Begin by asking students what it takes to be a superhero. Discuss as a class the necessary qualities and prerequisites. List as many superheroes as possible – both fictional and real-life. The answer is not clear cut, since even quite young children will recognise the idea of the anti-hero (in the form of the Hulk or of Batman – the Dark Knight version, for example).

Ask if comic-book superheroes are similar in any way to real-life celebrities and superstars. How, when, and why were *they* first created? Do we need to be cynical about the marketing machines that seek to manipulate our perceptions of famous people? See how many genuine real-life heroes the students can think of (people such as Neil Armstrong, Yuri Gagarin, Florence Nightingale etc.) and find out how much they know about them. Investigate why most children probably know more about, say Spider Man, than they do about these real heroes.

Once exploratory discussions are over, groups or individuals attempt to create a new superhero from scratch, leaning as little as possible on the characters created in books, comics and movies. Students should think about: name, costume (including colours and what they represent), logo, powers and abilities, reliance on technology versus mystical attributes, origins, lifestyle, companions, secret base and identity, etc. Would the character be a local or an international figure? Would s/he live in a real place or an hypothetical city such as Metropolis or Gotham? Could students begin to create a 'world picture' to accompany the vision of the hero/heroine (Batman's Gotham, for example, is dark and gloomy with a twist of madness). How much of the students' own opinions about good and evil are embodied in the character?

Extension activities/ variations

- Work could continue with stories, artwork, drama and so on, depicting the adventures of the new crusader for justice.
- Go on to explore and create a parallel character – **Supervillain**...

Linked activities

- Use the character templates *(Character Profile* and *Character Pyramid,* p.118-119) to explore the personality of your hero or heroine before designing him or her.

- Spend some time looking at the symbolic or metaphorical uses of colours and colour combinations (see *Symbols,* p.43). Look through books of symbols to help choose an appropriate logo for your superhero.

- Use the *Circles* template (p.47) for an in-depth look at your hero's thoughts and feelings, or have the template represent things happening in the environment your hero inhabits.

- Avoid stereotyping. Don't make your superhero entirely good and your supervillain entirely bad. Use the *Emotion Spectrum* activity (p.132) to help invest them with a blend of emotions.

Confucius-He-Say

GROUPING

Whole class or small groups

TIME

20 minutes

EQUIPMENT

Proverbs

This creative thinking game encourages students to 'unfold' good advice through discussion, and then to 'repackage' the wisdom they've learned in a pithy way. Aside from raising children's awareness of maxims and epithets and the metaphorical way in which they are often used, the act of children translating meanings into their own words allows them to experience the sense more forcefully.

Basic activity

Begin by looking at some simple, well-known mottoes, proverbs or sayings...

Do not cut down the tree that gives you shade.
All sunshine makes a desert.
Where there are fish, there must be water.
If a person could have half his wishes, he would double his troubles.
You should learn to sail in all winds.
No bird soars too high if he soars on his own wings.

Now choose a theme – perhaps one taken from the *Theme Card* bank (p.117), or one from another motto, or one which underlies a current topic of work: seasons, people and places, holidays, etc.

Explain the *Confucius* template, which for our purposes looks at both sides of the coin – the good and bad aspects of the chosen topic ...

> Confucius-he-say that falling leaves warn of winter snow (bad) and spring flowers (good).
>
> Confucius-he-say that the brightest light (good) casts the darkest shadow (bad).
>
> Confucius-he-say that the melting ice stops you skating (bad) but lets the ducks swim (good).
>
> Confucius-he-say cars make us go faster (good) but see less of the journey (bad).
>
> Confucius-he-say fire never learns lessons from us (bad), but we must always learn from fire (good).

Ask groups to attempt to create a saying in the style of Confucius, which in some way fits the chosen theme or picture. Suggest that groups find creative links by making free-association 'spidergrams' around the theme or item picked.

Confucius-he-say that the flower in the ground is more beautiful than the flower in the vase.

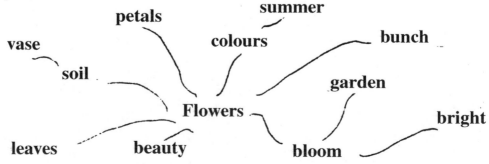

The only control the group-leader should exercise over the game is to steer students away from cliché.

If God Meant Us To Fly...

A variation of this activity is *If God Meant Us To Fly...* Ask learners if they are familiar with this idea – it is often used by adults to stop children from doing things that they enjoy!

- If God meant us to fly we would be born with landing gear, not legs.
- If God meant us to use typewriters He would have given us more fingers.
- If God meant us to go to war He would not have given us hearts.

The underlying theme of such mottoes is that to do anything which is regarded as out of the ordinary or abnormal is to break some higher law or authority. The aim of *If God Meant Us To Fly...* is not to be subversive, but to help define the boundaries of what is possible or acceptable.

Problem Page

GROUPING

Whole class / small groups

TIME

30-45 minutes

EQUIPMENT

Samples of problem page questions

Many children will be familiar with the 'agony aunt' column in comics and magazines. This activity aims to exploit the idea to allow students to raise issues and discuss problems more openly, and ultimately, to be self-supporting when it comes to seeking good advice.

Basic activity

1. Begin by introducing the activity to the whole class, explaining that they will be asked to discuss various 'problems' and find possible solutions. Then divide the class into groups.

2. Give each group a small selection of 'problems' to talk about and advise on. (The problems may have been generated earlier as a whole class exercise, or may have been gleaned from real magazine problem pages.)

3. After a reasonable time, redistribute the problems so that any given problem has been looked at by two groups.

4. Conclude the activity by bringing the class together. Read out problems chosen at random; ask the appropriate groups to offer their advice; then allow a brief brainstorming session before moving on to another issue.

NOTE

Specific areas of the curriculum can be targeted to generate material for the problems presented:

● Can you suggest an effective strategy to warn young people of the dangers of drugs?

● How can we (the parish council) solve the problem of litter in our village?

● How can I (a concerned parent) ensure that my children are not exposed to unsuitable material on TV and video?
And so on.

By giving students the responsibility of offering sound advice in this way, they develop an awareness of the issues more effectively than if they were 'told the facts' by some outside authority.

Penpals

This is a simple letter-writing activity that gives learners practice in both the fun and formalities of correspondence, allowing them to express their feelings, share ideas and concerns, and ask questions in a spirit of open-minded curiosity.

Basic activity

Students from within a group, or across the whole school, are paired off (by drawing names out of a hat, for example), and become pen pals for however long you want the activity to run. Vary the game by:

- maintaining anonymity between the letter-writers (false names and identities)
- involving children from other schools in the cluster
- setting up a real pen pal network with children abroad
- using *Circles* (p.47) or other character-generating games to invent fictitious personas
- asking one of the pair to pretend s/he's a famous personality

The obvious by-products of *Penpals* are fun and attention to detail in presenting written material; but friendships have been known to form as a result of the activity, and people tend to learn a lot about their correspondent, as well as about themselves.

GROUPING — Pairs

TIME — Slots of 15-20 minutes

EQUIPMENT — Quality stationery

Fuzwugs

| | GROUPING | Individual work / small groups |

Fuzwugs **popped into existence during a poetry workshop I was running with ten year-olds. We decided to create new creatures and then write poems about them.**

Basic activity

Begin by asking students to draw a 6x6 template. Along the top ask them to write down six characteristics (students can think of these themselves or use the ones given below). Ask them to number the characteristics 1-6 down the side and fill in spaces on the chart.

Now they are ready to begin creating fuzwugs. To do this they roll a dice six times, once for each characteristic. They may end up with, for example, a creature that is (dice roll: 3) metallic, (dice roll: 1) purple, (dice roll: 4) weightless, (dice roll: 5) huge, (dice roll: 1) round, and (dice roll: 2) lives on the moon.

	Texture	Colour	One Unique	Detail Size	Shape	Link Word
1	fluffy	purple	cheerful	tiny	round	bugs
2	smooth	green	gloomy	small	square	moon
3	metallic	yellow	hungry	medium	triangle	jungle
4	rough	orange	weightless	large	floppy	fly
5	silky	blue	mischievous	huge	thin	zoom
6	knobbly	red	different sizes	changes	flat	cats

Have learners draw their fuzwug and think of further attributes if they wish. Ask them to think up a name for their creature. The fuzwug can then be written about as a story, in verse, as a play, etc.

GROUPING Individual work / small groups

TIME 30 minutes

EQUIPMENT Paper, pencils, dice, drawing/ painting equipment

> "Out of clutter, find simplicity.
> From discord, find harmony.
> In the middle of difficulty,
> find opportunity"
>
> *Albert Einstein*

Section Seven

STORY MAKING

*T*he mind learns by creating significant connections between initially disparate pieces of information. Story making is therefore just one branch of this general 'meaning-making' process, and a normal, natural human ability. Stories of course are great fun – to read, listen to or write, and for this reason amongst others they also act a powerful vehicles for delivering information (see, for example, *Day To Day Parables*, p.127), or for packaging information. What we learn, either through formal curriculum content, or more broadly as we experience life, can be given further structure within a story. This, of course, is why most novelists follow the golden rule of 'writing what you know'.

To use stories to embody information and personal experience is a high level skill, but not beyond the capabilities of most children – when they feel comfortable and confident with the techniques of story making, within an environment which is non-judgmental, non-competitive, and which celebrates their individual achievement.

This section of the book offers strategies, techniques and activities to further the aims above. They have been used effectively with children of all ages and abilities, to enhance the skills learners already possess, and to introduce and bootstrap new skills within the enjoyable arena of story making.

Character Envelopes

GROUPING

Whole class / small groups

TIME

30 minutes upwards

EQUIPMENT

Envelopes, assorted small items (to put in envelopes)

This is a great activity for getting students to swap ideas. It allows children to ask open-ended questions, to brainstorm, and to make reasonable deductions based upon what they see. *Character Envelopes* **forms an effective way of allowing children to 'talk their way into a story'.**

Basic activity

1. Create a Character Envelope by selecting around six ordinary items at random – a bus ticket, an old watch, a comb, a food label, a stamp, a key – anything will do. Prepare enough envelopes to give out when the class is split into groups of four (smaller groups = more envelopes).

2. Do a whole-class demonstration using one envelope. Explain that the items inside are all connected; nobody yet knows exactly how, but they do all involve one person (an invented character to be made up as the game progresses).

3. Pick a couple of items out of the envelope and ask what they might suggest about the person involved – the comb, for instance, suggests s/he has hair, the bus ticket suggests this person uses public transport, and maybe can't afford a car.... Explain that these ideas are not 'right' or 'wrong', but may be more, or less, useful as the game goes on.

4. Continue to draw items out of the envelope, gathering and then modifying ideas about the character.

5. Distribute the remaining envelopes, split the class into groups, and have them run through the process again, this time on their own.

6. Subsequently, ask groups to feed back information about their characters. This information could be kept in the form of a *Character Profile* or *Character Pyramid* (see p.118-119), and could later be used as a 'Character Bank' when stories are written.

Extension activities/ variations

- Ask groups to construct character envelopes of their own, by bringing in items from home (asking permission first!), or selecting objects from around the classroom and/or *Sundries Bag* (p.17). They could base their envelopes on well-known personalities. What would the Sherlock Holmes' envelope contain, for example?

- Have individuals construct character envelopes of themselves – selecting objects that give clues to their identity without revealing too much. Then ask them to swap anonymously and try to work out the owner of the envelope they're given.

- Each group, or each individual in a group, contributes one item to go in the envelope, then discussion focuses on the character implied by the selection.

If materials are short or hard to obtain ("But sir, I don't have a Rolex Oyster Perpetual or a Walther PPK!"), then the activity can be done entirely on paper. Easier, but not so much fun.

Linked activities

The *Circles* activity (p.47) could be used to flesh-out characters before beginning this game.

Mix And Match Titles

Prepare a list of a hundred or so book titles (large print). Cut up the titles and mix them. Have small groups match up different combinations to create new titles which can then act as springboards for stories, poems and plays.

Soap Opera

GROUPING

Whole class

TIME

Variable. A short 20-30 minute session or a large topic spread over several lessons.

EQUIPMENT

None

Most of us are familiar with at least one 'soap' on TV, radio, or in comics. This activity exploits that interest by having a whole class create their own soap opera scenario, complete with characters, streets (or a whole town!) and possible storylines. Not only is this an effective way of making up stories, but the activity can also act as a vehicle to raise, discuss and perhaps resolve real-life issues and concerns.

Basic activity

1. As a whole class, begin by making basic decisions about the soap. Where will it be set? In a real place or a made-up locale? Discuss the basic details of the environment. Decide on a reasonable number of main characters, not too many or too few, and just attach a few details to each character or group of characters (e.g. the Jessup family: Mum, Dad, and four kids – three girls and a boy. They're untidy, boisterous, but very friendly and seem to be really close and to enjoy life). Decisions can be made through discussion and/or rolling the dice (as described in *Dice Journey*, p.177).

2. Prepare a simple drawing of the locale, incorporating ideas from the whole class. For plans of individual houses, you could split the class into groups and have them sketch rooms and gardens. Using pictures from magazines, catalogues etc. as reference materials may be helpful.

3. Flesh out characters by using, for example the *Circles* template (p.47), or by running the *Character Envelopes* game (p.154).

4. Now begin to develop storylines. At first, use ideas to be found in 'real' soaps – pinch and adapt freely, perhaps using the *Story Tree* template (p.168). By discussing the reactions of the different characters to situations as they evolve, plots can emerge in an 'organic' way.

5. When characters and ongoing storylines are developed to some extent, introduce issues that you feel it appropriate or necessary to discuss. By having the soap characters experience and cope with these situations, the children in the class are distanced from possibly sensitive material; they can learn from the characters' reactions; and feel confident in giving views and ideas which in that sense are 'not their own'.

Extension activities/ variations

The form that *Soap Opera* takes in the classroom can vary. The ongoing characters and situations might be visited on a regular basis for the purposes of discussion work, or to practise a linked skill (writing dialogue, point-of-view work, etc.). Or the activity could be more intensive, over several consecutive 'lessons', leading to a piece of drama or script-writing, perhaps forming the basis of a presentation in assembly or book week.

Linked activities

- You could use *Spidergrams* (p.46) to help develop the characters and relationships in the soap opera.

- Once location, characters and perhaps broad themes and general storylines have been discussed, use the *Dice Journey* technique (p.177) to introduce random elements of narrative structure. Develop the best of these into more formal and extended pieces of work.

Random Paragraphs

Take a short story and cut it up into sections. Have groups reconstitute the story. Or give different groups a separate section and ask them to make up the missing portions of the narrative.

Genre Chart

GROUPING

Whole class / small groups

TIME

20-30 minutes

EQUIPMENT

Examples of different genres (in literature, art, drama etc..)

Genre Chart **allows students to explore conventions and motifs within a genre; to become more aware of stereotypes; and to investigate interesting areas for creative thinking where genres overlap.**

The principles of *Genre Chart* **need not be confined to literature: all forms of art can be looked at in this way, and it can also be adapted for other curriculum areas such as Media Education, PSE, and so on.**

Basic activity

1. Ask the groups to think of as many different genres of fiction as possible: Horror, Science Fiction, Fantasy, Romance, Spy, Murder Mystery, Westerns, Crime, Historical, War (note that ideas like Animal Stories, Comedy, Adventure etc. could be classed as genres in their own right, or as elements within a genre story – so you could have a Comedy Science Fiction, an Adventure Thriller, a Fantasy with animal characters, etc.)

2. Now gather ideas about the kinds of characters, objects ('props') and situations you might find within any chosen genre. Use ideas from books, comics, TV, etc. For example, taking Fantasy, the key elements would be:

Characters – wizards, dragons, trolls, enchanters, unicorns...
Objects – magic crystals, wands, swords with special powers, secret boxes...
Situations – overcoming guardians of the gate, entering an enchanted forest, choosing between two alternatives, conversing with a magical being, setting out on a quest...

3. Once the basic idea of the activity has been grasped, students could go on to:
- List the features of the character types they would find in different genres. For example, in a detective story you might find: the loyal assistant who's slightly slow on the uptake, the quirky but brilliant solver of crimes, the thoroughly evil and scheming master villain, the thuggish and stupid henchmen, etc...
- Devise some typically genre-based titles for stories. A good way of doing this is to collect titles that already exist and 'ring the changes'. Notice what makes a good title, the kinds of ideas that commonly occur, repeated words and concepts. Have a brainstorming session as a first step towards making a final title. A good title keeps the writer to the point of the story, and is dramatic and eye-catching for the reader.
- Illustrate the style, 'flavour' or characteristics of a genre visually, using collage, abstract art, etc.
- Select a picture, story extract or piece of music which illustrates for them the main characteristics of a chosen genre.
- Discuss ways in which genres can be combined to break new ground or give well-worn ideas a new twist. E.g., Horror Westerns, Science Fiction Spy Stories, Crime Fantasies.
- Develop a piece of art, dance, drama, etc. to illustrate the major motifs of a chosen genre.
- Create a multi-media presentation to explain a genre to an audience coming fresh to the idea.
- Prepare a parody of a chosen genre, presenting it in any form you like.

Genre Chart

(Romance, science fiction, war, spy, fantasy, western, horror, crime, historical, etc.).

Genre

Themes

Motifs

Characters

Objects

Events

Deconstruction

GROUPING	Whole class
TIME	20-30 minutes
EQUIPMENT	None

Sometimes you need to take things apart to understand how they work – or to put them together in a new way. The word for this process is *deconstruction*. It can be used in many contexts, though its most obvious application is in the Arts, including English and Media Studies.

The activity works well in the planning stages of the writing process, and to enhance storytelling skills.

Basic activity

Begin by telling a familiar story, such as *Little Red Riding Hood*. Now, with the class, write each part of the story, each main event, as a brief phrase or sentence:

1. Red Riding Hood is sent to take food to her grandmother, who's ill.
2. Red Riding Hood walks through the wood and meets the wolf.
3. The wolf chats with Red Riding Hood and asks her where she is going.
4. The wolf races ahead, eats up the grandmother, and dresses in her clothes.
5. Red Riding Hood arrives and thinks that grandma looks strange.
6. The wolf reveals itself and threatens to eat up Red Riding Hood.
7. The woodcutter arrives, kills the wolf in time and out pops grandma (depending on which version you read!).

Once you have 'deconstructed' the story like this, there are various ways to develop the activity:

- Explore the larger themes (in this case, the dark unknown woods, danger disguised in innocence, the naive and vulnerable child). In which other stories do these themes occur? Do we meet them in real life?

- Look at stereotyping and ask *What If?* questions.... What if the wolf had been a lion? What if Red Riding Hood had been a boy or if she had been a nasty character? What if the woodcutter had been a woman? Would the outcome of the story have been different?

- See how the story fits into other times, places, genres. Imagine *Little Red Riding Hood* as a futuristic Science Fiction story for example, or a contemporary romance story or a *Lord of the Rings*-style fantasy, and discuss how the elements of the story (characters, situations, etc.) might have to change.

Now split the class into groups. Give each group one chunk of the story and ask them to elaborate upon it, putting in more descriptive details, more dialogue, thinking of the story from a different point of view (first person as the wolf, grandma, woodcutter, maybe).

Extension activities/ variations

Once students have become familiar with 'deconstruction' techniques, move on to more complex stories and/ or encourage them to use the techniques when they look back over stories they themselves have written.

Linked activities

Use the tale as the basis for a *Story Tree* (p.168).

Mythologies

Take a natural phenomenon and (whether the group understands the scientific basis of it or not), devise mythical stories to explain it. Why does the moon have phases? What makes thunder and lightning? Why do some people have fair hair and some have dark hair? Why do rainbows sometimes appear after showers?

The output of ideas can be used for stories, music, drama, art, or as a way of highlighting the scientific facts behind the phenomenon.

Dialogue Sheet

GROUPING

Class demonstration, followed by work in pairs or small groups

TIME

15-20 minutes

EQUIPMENT

Dialogue sheet templates

This is another template for creative thinking. An endless range of dialogue sheets such as the one shown here can be created, and used in a wide variety of contexts, not necessarily English Literature / Language based. For instance, use the template to invent conversations between famous historical figures/ between people from different cultures or with different views/ between famous scientists (whether or not they actually ever met or talked doesn't matter!).

Basic activity

Photocopy the dialogue sheet opposite and give a copy to each member of the class/group. Explain that the punctuation marks for an imaginary conversation have been written out, but the words themselves are missing. The task is to supply those missing words, together with any notes on intonation or other qualities of the voice.

Decide on the theme or topic for the conversation, together with what kind of mood the 'characters' might be in. For instance, if you were using the template to explore the issue of, say, the way films are rated (U, PG, 12, 18), character A might be a child who wants to go in to see a movie but is too young; character B might be an older friend who supports her/his view; a third character (C) might be the cinema manager who is determined not to see the rules broken. A's mood is defiant and angry, B's mood is firm and reasonable, C's mood is impatient and snappy.

Extension activities/ variations

Once you've run the basic activity, you might try the following:

● Swap filled-in templates between groups for different views and feedback.

● Use dialogue sheets as the basis for further class discussion and debate.

● Insert dialogue sheets where appropriate into stories.

● Incorporate information (i.e. syllabus content) into more elaborate dialogues. Base the dialogue on a topic you've been studying in class.

Linked activities

● To fix the scenario firmly in students' minds, consider using character generating templates such as *Character Pyramid* (p.119) or *Circles* (p.47).

Dialogue sheet template

1) _____ _____ _____ – _____ , _____ .

2) " _____ ! _____ _____ _____ _____ _____ ."

3) " _____ _____ ____ _____ _____ . _____ _____ ?"

4) " _____ _____ _____ _____ , _____ ... "

5) " _____ ' ___ , _____ _____ ."

6) " _____ ?"

7) " _____ _____ _____ : _____ _____ _____ .... ?"

8) " _____ – _____ !"

9) " ' _____ _____ _____ _____ _____ .' _____ _____ ____ ."

10) " _____ _____ !"

Horoscopes And Fortunes

The language of mass media horoscopes is wonderfully vague and unfailingly optimistic (though with little threads of warning woven here and there). Apart from writing horoscopes themselves as a creative exercise you could use variations on the theme to extend students, thinking skills.

Basic activities

- Have students bring horoscopes to school and use the incidents they suggest for story writing, drama or art.
- Use join-the-dots techniques to make up some new Zodiacal constellations; invent the mythology around them; devise the personality-types linked with those birth signs.
- Analyse the language structures of horoscopes and write some for fictitious characters.

Linked activities

- You could use horoscopes and/or the attributes supposedly linked with birth signs (e.g. Capricorns are meant to be good humoured, attractive, popular and intelligent) with *Character Profiles, Character Pyramids* (p.118-119) or *Circles* (p.47) as a basis for generating characters for stories.

Fortunes

This activity involves the use of numbers linked with a general statement about how the future might turn out. The idea can be adapted for use in story making.

Begin by writing the numbers 1-26 onto separate pieces of paper. Now ask groups to pick out say four pieces of paper each. Choose a theme, genre and characters for a story and ask groups to discuss how, when, where and why the messages on the pieces of paper might feature in the story.

1   - *consider your needs and the environment.*
2   - *partnerships are likely.*
3   - *be sensitive to signals and coincidence.*
4   - *it's time for a parting or separation.*
5   - *be strong and determined now.*
6   - *you are about to break into new areas.*
7   - *things happen to limit you.*
8   - *you move into a fertile environment.*
9   - *look to your defences.*
10 - *to protect now will prevent trouble later.*
11 - *possessions become more important.*
12 - *joy is coming to you soon.*
13 - *soon you will reap the harvest of your efforts.*
14 - *openings lie ahead.*
15 - *if you want something, be prepared to fight for it.*

GROUPING
Whole class/ small groups

TIME
20-30 minutes

EQUIPMENT
None

16 - *this is a time of new growth.*

17 - *move on and see obstacles removed.*

18 - *don't fight, just go along with circumstances.*

19 - *everything is about to suffer disturbance.*

20 - *important messages are about to arrive.*

22 - *be patient, you stand on a threshold.*

23 - *a difficult problem is solved.*

24 - *events stand still, so be patient.*

25 - *the whole thing; look at it again.*

26 - *the unknown – wait and see.*

Extension activities/ variations

Another way of using the above idea is to write out the messages themselves onto strips of paper and encourage students during story making to pick one out at random as a stimulus to further ideas.

Storyboarding

GROUPING

Whole class/
small groups

TIME

30 minutes
upwards

EQUIPMENT

Storyboard
templates,
OHP (optional)

Before a film is ever made, the story is drawn out as a storyboard, a kind of comic-strip format which gives insights into structuring action sequences, assessing camera angles, anticipating later difficulties, and so on.

This technique can be utilised in helping students to plan their own stories – and you don't need to be able to draw – matchstick people work just as well as more artistically executed figures.

Basic activity

Explain to learners that this is a story-making activity that will help them both to visualise and plan their stories with greater clarity and detail.

Run a class demonstration (using an OHP if possible).
1. Decide on a story, or a portion of a story, to be 'storyboarded'.
2. Show the class a storyboarding template (see p.167) and explain the principle behind it (see above).
3. Make sure students have an idea about which characters are featured, and something of the context of the piece being worked on.
4. Work on the first panel of the storyboard. The first panel of the storyboard doesn't need to correspond to the start of the story. The board storyline has already been discussed by this stage, so teacher and pupils will have a fair idea of what Panel One would show. Decide which characters are present. How are they positioned in relation to one another? What are they saying? (Keep it brief). What has happened earlier in the story to bring them to this point? What might happen now?
5. Add details by looking at the colours that could feature in the panel, the sounds, smells and textures, etc. Create a multi-sensory experience.

Work through a few other panels in the same way, then have small groups finish the storyboard and/or work on their own ideas using fresh templates. The idea is to represent the story's plot, or part of it, in visual form, however crudely. Thus, panels will show characters interacting with each other and the location. There'll be speech bubbles, notes on colours and sounds, etc. Small boxes might be used for close-ups or to show small details; large boxes allow space for more to be happening. Look at a cartoon comic to see how panelling is used in this way.

Extension activities/ variations

● Paste a single frame from a comic strip story on to a storyboard template and have groups fill out the rest of the tale.

● Storyboard a portion of a favourite film or novel.

Linked activities

● Generate characters before storyboarding using, for example, the *Character Pyramid* (p.119) or *Circles* (p.47) technique.

● Develop the landscape of the story by using the *Map Maker* game (p.80).

● Initial plotting can help the *Storyboard* game to run more smoothly – use *Dice Journey* (p.177) or *Story Tree* (p.168) for this.

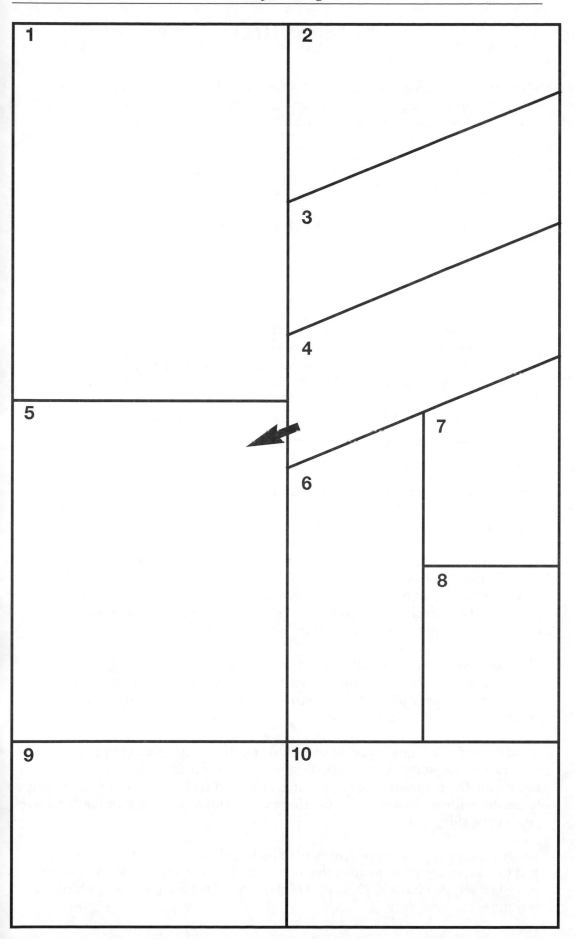

Story Tree

GROUPING
Small group/
pair or
individual
work

TIME
30 minutes
upwards

EQUIPMENT
Dice, sugar
panel,
colouring
pencils and a
spinner

**Many people approach stories in a linear way: children are taught that stories
have a beginning, a middle and an end... And so they do, *when they are
finished*. At the outset though – during the thinking time – ideas can come
along from any part of the narrative. Ideally, the student's evolving idea of the
story should accommodate the natural flow of ideas (all ideas, not just good
ones) and incorporate an overview of all of the possibilities for that story.
Story Tree hopefully achieves these aims.**

Story Tree **is a key activity, insofar as it can draw together many of the other
creative tools in this book.**

Basic activity

Begin with a starting-point for a story – this could be inspired by a picture, a
proverb, a symbol, a *context sentence* (see p.90), an item or two from the *Sundries
Bag* (p.17), or objects brought in by the children. Use this stimulus as the 'seed'
from which any number of stories can grow.

Preliminary discussion can focus on exploring the immediate context...

- How many people are there in the story at this point?
- What do they look like?
- What do the immediate surroundings look like?

Now ask, what might happen next.

The group needs to take a decision about which of the story 'branches' to
develop first. Discussion follows on the chosen strand until plot events dictate a
further split, and another decision needs to be taken about which of those
possible 'sub-branches' to follow first. Students record the development, either
on a tree diagram (if they are brief) or in note books.

The story unfolds through discussion, dice rolls, or whatever, until either that
narrative strand reaches a natural conclusion, or a dead end, or until ideas run
out. Students then backtrack to an earlier branch of the tree in order to follow
another line of thinking.

Steadily, and often quite quickly using this method, a number of options for
structuring the story are developed – a network of possible storylines. This
represents the planning stage of writing, achieved without the ordeal of trying
to generate ideas out of thin air or struggle on with a flagging plot that's taking
you in one direction only.

The finished story tree allows writers to pick and choose the strongest storyline,
and to take elements from abandoned branches where applicable. Writing the
story is then seen for what it is, part of the larger creative process of Thinking –
Writing – Looking Back.

Example (Three children are lost in a hotel.....)

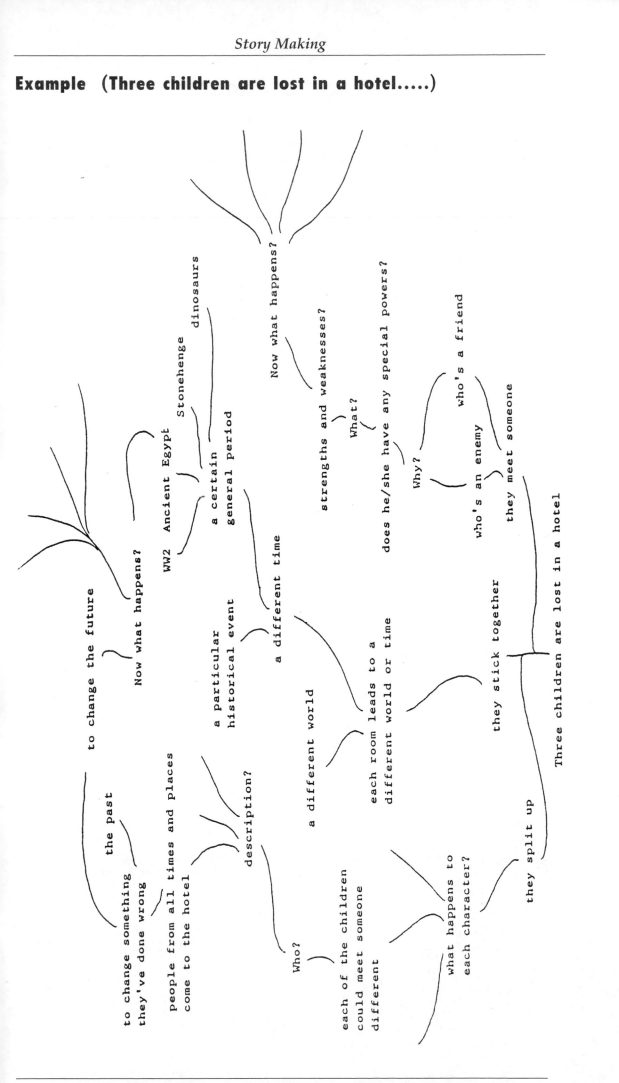

The mind map contains the following words and phrases:

Now what happens?

dinosaurs
Stonehenge
Ancient Egypt
WW2

a certain general period

Now what happens?

strengths and weaknesses?

What?

does he/she have any special powers?

who's a friend

Why?

who's an enemy

they meet someone

to change the future

the past

a particular historical event

a different time

a different world

each room leads to a different world or time

they stick together

Three children are lost in a hotel

to change something they've done wrong

people from all times and places come to the hotel

description?

they split up

Who?

each of the children could meet someone different

what happens to each character?

Control Panel

GROUPING

Small groups
or pair work

TIME

15-20 minutes

EQUIPMENT

Control panel
template

This is a useful device for visualisation, and/or for allowing students to make imaginative leaps forward when reviewing material they've already written. The purpose of the device is to make students aware of the degree of control they can have over their own work, by becoming sensitive to different aspects of the writing.

Basic activity

Construct a template (such as the one shown on p.171) using On/Off switches, sliders, knobs and buttons. Explain to the group that each control mechanism can alter, add or remove something from, say, a story or piece of factual writing. The controls on the panel could perhaps include:

- dials that relate to the five senses
- a positive/negative switch
- a slider that can be applied to emotions
- a balancing knob between dialogue and narrative
- a volume control for dialogue
- a 'time switch' to increase or decrease the pace of the writing
- a 'detail dial' to alter work which is overwritten or underwritten

Explain to students that once a story has been written, it is not 'set in stone'. A story (or a poem, description, picture, piece of music, etc.) is simply made of ideas, which can be changed. *Control Panel* forms part of the 'looking back' phase of story making.

In small groups or pairs, ask students to think about what would happen – how the writing could change – if one dial or switch or button on the Control Panel was adjusted. Illustrate with a simple example. Suppose a piece of writing did not mention any colours. Turn up the 'colour dial' a bit. Where could colour be mentioned?

Once students have the idea, they can experiment with other controls (i.e. parameters of writing), discussing within their groups or as a whole class the results they have discovered.

- This technique works wonderfully if students have access to computers, where text files can be duplicated and altered within moments.
- Control panels can be constructed with particular kinds of writing in mind, and at a level appropriate to differing ages and abilities.

Example:

Before:

"Rockfall!" Tim yelled. He took his sister's hand and they ran. The noise was deafening, and clouds of dust filled the air.

Together Tim and Teena ran towards the only shelter – their father's Time Platform. There they crouched while rocks fell about them and soil piled around their ankles.

After a minute or so it was all over. Teena looked out from her hiding place and saw that the rock-fall was almost over.

"I think we're safe," she said, but then a stray stone hit Professor Taylor's computer, and a strange sound began. A bright light flashed around the children and then, out of nowhere, a weird kind of doorway opened.

Tim opened his mouth in amazement, as the light grew brighter and the ground began to move...

Tim and Teena stepped on to the platform, holding on to each other in fright.

Soon the light began to fade and they could smell a jungle smell. Suddenly there was a screech. The children looked up and their mouths dropped open. A great dragon-like creature was sailing by.

"I think," Teena said quietly, "we've just done what Dad told us not to. We've transported ourselves to the Age of the Dinosaurs..."

Control Panel:

SOUND KNOB

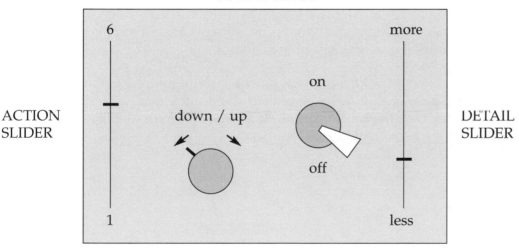

COLOUR SWITCH

Steve: OK Neil, read through that bit of work again and tell me where you think the control panel settings are at the moment...

Neil: Um, Action Slider about 3... What do you mean by Sound Knob?

Steve: The number of times you mention sounds, instead of just telling the reader that sounds were happening. I mean, actually saying what the sounds were.

Neil: OK... I think the Sound Knob is turned down at the moment.

Steve: Right, so if you turned it up your story would mention sounds more often, and you'd have a greater *range* of sounds. What about the Colour Switch?

Neil: Off. I've hardly mentioned the colours of things.

Steve: OK, but it's easy to look at some of the things you've put in your story, and give them colours... The clouds of dust, the bright light, the dragon-like creature...

Neil: Yes. And I'll push up the Detail Slider too, so I can put a bit more description in...

Steve: You go ahead and alter those controls, then keep the new settings in mind as you alter your work. Then we'll see how it reads...

After:-

"Rockfall!" Tim yelled. He grabbed his sister's hand and ran. The noise was deafening. There was a huge roar and clouds of orange dust filled the air.

Together Tim and Teena ran towards the only shelter – their father's Time Platform. There they crouched while rocks banged and clanged on the metal and soil piled around their ankles.

After a minute or so the terrible drumming grew less. Teena peeped out from her hiding place and saw that the rock-fall was almost over.

"I think we're safe," she said with a gasp of relief. But then a stray stone hit Professor Taylor's computer, and a strange deep humming began. A bright white light flashed around them and there, right out of nowhere, a doorway opened – a swirling doorway into time.

Tim opened his mouth in amazement. But then the Platform's power reached its peak. The light became blinding. There was a BANG and the ground began to move.

Tim and Teena scrambled on to the platform, clinging to each other in terror.

Soon the bright light began to fade and they could smell a warm, damp, earthy smell. It was the smell of jungle trees, water and mud. They could hear the sounds of leaves in the wind... And then a screech like iron scraping on tin.

The children looked up and their mouths dropped open. A great, black, leathery, dragon-like creature was sailing by. It was as big as an aeroplane.

"I think," Teena said quietly, "we've just done what Dad told us not to. We've transported ourselves to the Age of the Dinosaurs..."

The usefulness of *Control Panel* is that it allows young writers to focus on individual aspects of their work, and instead of feeling that they're being criticised, they can take control of the situation themselves to make the changes that we, the teachers, think are necessary.

Minisagas

GROUPING
Class demonstration followed by individual or pair work

TIME
20-30 minutes

EQUIPMENT
None

This is a wonderful idea which I first heard about on BBC Radio 4. A minisaga is a story of *exactly* 50 words, excluding the title, which can be up to 14 words long. I used to pull this exercise out of the hat when my classes complained about written assignments being too long – or to answer the perennial question, 'But sir, how long does the story have to be?'

Results can be highly entertaining, and the stories themselves can be generated by using a range of techniques in this book, such as those listed below, or by adapting traditional stories such as fairytales.

Basic activity

Explain to the group that their task is to tell the chosen story using precisely 50 words. Their stories must include the main building blocks of the story – character(s), background, beginning-middle-end etc. – and so great thought must be put into choosing the right words, then editing down (or up) those words to fit the frame.

- Read out an example of a minisaga, such as the one below.
  Two rival explorers were hunting for rare butterflies in the jungle . Suddenly both saw the flicker of rainbow wings and hurried to capture this beautiful specimen. Their nets swished but became tangled. At that, they began to argue and fight, while the angel looked on in amazement, before flying away.

- Suggest that students can use stories or ideas they have heard before – or you may wish to use a picture, proverb, page from a comic book, etc. as the focus instead.

- Emphasise that you don't need to hit the 50-word target on the first writing; write the story as briefly as you can, and then edit down (or up!).

- Encourage students to do more than construct an 'and then...' list.

- Once the activity has been run, ask for results to be read out.

TIP If students find the task too difficult, introduce an overlap of +/- 10% words.

NOTE Writing minisagas is a cumulative skill. Try it several times to ensure that students get the idea that good writing is a matter of getting the words to do the work.

Extension activities/ variations

● Vary the activity by introducing sagas of different lengths:
  - microsagas – 25 words
  - midisagas – 100 words
  - maxisagas – 250 words
  - megasagas – 500 words

Another variation of this activity is *Picture Postcard*. Students are given a blank postcard-size piece of card or paper. On one side they must describe the view the postcard is supposed to show; on the other they comment on the highlights of their holiday.

Linked activities

Activities such as *Dice Journey* (p.177), *Proverbs* (p.175) and *Freeze-frame* (p.71) are useful for creating stories, which can then be turned into minisagas.

Proverbs

GROUPING — Whole class / small groups

TIME — 30 minutes

EQUIPMENT — List of proverbs (see p.186)

Proverbs provide a useful and effective stimulus for story making. They are, if you like, tightly-wrapped packages of ideas and wisdom, which can be 'unfolded' and manipulated in a variety of ways...

Basic activities

Ask students to think of proverbs that they have heard (see examples on p.186). You could follow on with a variety of activities:

- Suggest alternative explanations for extant proverbs. For example:
  'A cheerful look makes a dish a feast' could mean:
  - If the chef and waiter look happy, people relish their food more.
  - If the restaurant is colourful and clean, people enjoy their food more.
  - People respond more positively if something looks cheerful – a smiling person, a brightly decorated room, a sunny day, a colourfully presented piece of work, etc.

- Create new proverbs.

- Discuss real-life examples of the truth of proverbs (but don't get too personal!). For example:
  'Hasty climbers have sudden falls':
  - Our window cleaner tried to hurry up his ladder and spilled his water.
  - My Uncle Jim rushed to catch the train, bumped into a lady and knocked her bag on the floor. By the time he'd helped her and apologised, he'd missed the train.
  - Sara's little brother Darren wanted to have a bicycle like hers. His mum said he had to use the stabilisers, but Darren thought he could ride the bike without them. He pestered Mum until she took them off. When he first tried to ride, he fell off and grazed his knee.

- Connect proverbs with particular emotions. For example:
  - *'When the cat's away the mice will play'* – mischief.
  - *'Fire is a good servant but a bad master'* – fear, awe, respect.
  - *'Enough is better than too much'* – greed.
  - *'Better to be alone than in bad company'* – foolishness, unhappiness.

- Time-hop into the future and invent suitable new proverbs that refer to the world as it is in, say, the year 3000.

Linked activities

- Link *Proverbs* with *A Day In The Life* (p.131). For example, *A Day In The Life Of A Traindriver*:
  - *'A miss is as good as a mile'* (passengers missing the train).
  - *'Absence makes the heart grow fonder '*(homesickness)
  - *'As you make your bed, so you must lie on it '*(attitude to the job).
  - *'Better late than never!'*

- Look at *Ladder To The Moon* (p.183). Find a proverb that matches, or suggests a link, with each category of story in the ladder. – i.e., is there a proverb that suggests an ancestor story, a creation myth, etc.

- Use a proverb as the initial premise for a *Story Tree* (p.168) or *Dice Journey* (p.177).

- Use proverbs as a basis for *Day-To-Day Parables* (p.127) by seeing if any proverbs sum up or explain a chosen parable. E.g. *The Backwards Walking Traveller*:
  - '*A person is as old as s/he feels.*'
  - '*A wise man changes his mind sometimes, a fool never.*'
  - '*Advice when most needed is least heeded.*'
  - '*Lost time is never found.*'

Superstitions

- Take a theme – such as 'wood' – and find as many superstitions as possible connected with it, or invent new ones.
- Select some obscure superstitions (taking the last piece of bread from a communal plate brings good luck, for example) and suggest a variety of reasonable explanations for it.
- Take a superstition as the initial premise for a *Story Tree* (p.168) or a *Circles* (p.47) exercise to generate a character or scenario.

Dice Journey

GROUPING
Class demonstration, splitting into groups of 3-6

TIME
1 hour upwards

EQUIPMENT
Dice, coloured counters, A1 – size paper, marker pens

This is a central activity insofar as it draws together so many other games and devices from *Imagine That...* It began as a story-making workshop, and I still use it as such; but it can be adapted in various ways for a range of purposes.

Playing the game as a story making device serves all the purposes of the thinking stage of story making, without the difficulties of trying to 'invent stories out of thin air', and without the unpopular connotations of 'planning' and 'drafting'. The experience engages students imaginatively in the process of thinking about plot, characters and background in a social and enjoyable way. The actual writing is fairly minimal, and the game is non-threatening, so unconfident children can play a full part in the generation and evolution of ideas.

At least (or at worst!) *Dice Journey* gives children an hour of noisy fun. But ultimately it is a means to the end of giving students a way of being enthusiastic about writing fiction, and a range of techniques for exploiting that enthusiasm to the full.

Basic activity

All you need for the basic *Dice Journey* are some large sheets of paper (A1 size is ideal), marker pens, coloured counters and dice. The game works best in small groups, though I have run the workshop with whole classes (and once with three classes together!) by using a flipchart and OHP.

To run the game as a story making device, proceed as follows:

Explain that shortly we'll be going on a journey. Right now we don't know where, or when or with whom – or even what kind of journey it will be. It isn't even certain that we'll be 'stepping into' the game at the start of the journey. But none of that really matters, because if we get stuck we can always ask 'The Boss' for advice.

The Boss, of course, is the dice. We only roll the dice if we absolutely can't agree on what to do, or if we want to introduce an unexpected element into the journey. Once we've asked The Boss for advice or a decision, we have to abide by it (unless there are special circumstances, such as the answer contradicting some previous decision, or if the 'advice' makes it impossible to continue with the journey).

The dice can be used in many ways, but a basic function is to say: 1-3 = Yes; 4-6 = No. There is a 1 – 6 scale, where 1 is Low and 6 is High. (Polyhedral dice can be used to roll higher numbers where required, and coloured dice are handy when doing character work – see p.178. No.6.)

Before beginning the dice journey, preliminary decisions have to be taken, by consensus or dice rolls.

1. What kind of story shall we make – i.e. what genre? (See pages 158 and 159.)
2. Will it be a serious story, or have a comedy element (1-6 scale dice roll, or a straight Yes/No decision).

3. Where will the story take place?

4. When will the story take place – that is, the time when we 'step into' the story – period in history, time of year, time of day etc.

5. We need to have a sense of location, of what's all around us as we step into the story. To achieve this, draw the cardinal compass points in a corner of a sheet of paper (or the blackboard). Put a small X in the centre of the sheet, and ask the members of the group to imagine they are standing there. Look to the north – what can you see? Write this down or draw it, then fill in the other directions.

6. We need to think about characters now. How many characters will there be when we step into the story? (Dice roll 1-6; any more than six characters makes the game very unwieldy, especially at the outset). OK, how many of you (group members) want to take on the role of one of these characters? (Dice roll to determine which group members are attached to 'player characters'.) Player characters can either 'be themselves' in the story, or role-play a generated character. In this case, each student will still be responsible for his/her character when it comes to making decisions, putting words into the character's mouth etc. 'Role play' in this sense means engaging imaginatively with the character and his/her world; although improvised drama can prove a fruitful way of doing this. The other characters in the story will remain non-player characters. Non-player characters are created and disposed of in the story as appropriate, to serve whatever purpose. Decisions about their appearance, personality and behaviour are taken through discussion, or by allowing the dice to choose.

   The characters will evolve during the story. Allocate a colour to each character. If characters need to be chosen to do particular things ("OK, which one of us is going into the dark tunnel first?"), roll the colour dice if agreement can't otherwise be reached. Colour dice can also be used if pairs or groups of characters need to work together.

Having decided the basics – what, where, when and who – you can begin to add structure to the story itself.

7. Roll the dice on the 1-6 scale to see at what point we join the narrative. Roll 1 and we begin at the beginning; roll 3 and we join the action half way through. In the case of any number except 1, we'll need to work backwards to some extent to discover what brought us to the point at which we entered the story.

8. Involve participants imaginatively in the story at this point. Encourage them to assume the role of their characters, and/or discuss the viewpoints of non-player characters. Feed the imagination by introducing a picture or music stimulus, or by asking questions about what they can see, hear, smell, etc.

Once groups have a broad idea of the context in which they step into the story, you can then ask the 'kick-start' question, *What Happens Next?* If ideas are not forthcoming, use the dice to make decisions. Which way shall we go? Shall we split up? Something's happening over there, what is it?

As participants become more involved and accumulate information, encourage the use of a *Story Tree* template (see p.168) to keep track of ideas and narrative avenues already explored. If groups begin to fragment because individuals or pairs want to go off in different directions, you can let them do this because the work already done and the use of the dice-as-arbiter keeps the activity under control.

Extension activities/ variations

There are many ways of exploiting the material generated during the *Dice Journey* activity:

- Character details, plot structures, pieces of dialogue, particular sentences, can be written-up and put into the resource banks. *(Picture Bank, Card Bank, Word Bank, Theme Bank).*

- Neatly drawn journeys can be given to other groups who are then asked to flesh out the story skeleton.

- *Dice Journey* can also be linked with topics in art, drama, music; or given particular emphasis so that other subjects/ areas of the curriculum are brought in. For example, insist that a journey is set in, say, Africa, so facts about landscape, animals, climate, etc., need to be researched and used. Or try a dice journey in Shakespeare's England, or one in which moral and ethical choices need to be made, and relevant issues explored.

- Dice journeys with logic, mathematical or language-oriented puzzles and quizzes form another possibility, though would need greater planning.

You can also vary or add to dice journeys in the following ways:

- Number a set of pictures. Roll polyhedral dice to determine the sequence, then ask groups to construct a dice journey to create a narrative link through the sequence.

- Devise a set of Chance Cards that pose generalised problems, conflicts or crises. For example:
  - Introduce a new character now.
  - You experience a change in fortunes within five minutes.
  - There's a disagreement in your story now.
  - You meet sudden danger.
  - You take a risk within five minutes.
  - A stranger arrives.
  - Something wanted and something unwanted come into your story now.
  - You suffer a sudden setback.
  - Good fortune comes your way.

  Players must put these into context as they work through the journey. Either the teacher or the students can decide when the chance cards are picked. I usually stick to something simple, like when a six is thrown.

- Write out 'Prompt Cards' as a variation on helping players who seem to run out of momentum:
  - Where are we?
  - What can we see as we look N/E/S/W?
  - Which way do we go?
  - What sounds can we hear?
  - Something's happening right now...What is it? How do we deal with it?

- Strike a balance between the spontaneity of *Dice Journey* and the more considered creation of stories by providing a workbook. At certain points in the journey, players would be required to write-up their experiences in a systematic way – e.g.: describe your character (for this students could use the *Character Sheet / Character Pyramid* templates on p.118-119), or write a diary of the day's events, etc. Alternatively they could record their work as a collection of fragments that could be drawn together at a later stage.

- Use *Dice Journey* for oral work. In the past, the activity has successfully formed the basis of GCSE oral assessments in English.

Linked activities

- Students could use the *Circles* device (p.47) to flesh-out the characters in the dice journey.

- Other games like *Dialogue Sheet* (p.162) and *Storyboarding* (p.166) can be used to focus students' attention on particular aspects of the story or the writing process, if in their excitement they have skipped over details in the dice journey itself.

- Use *Abstract Art* (p.43) or *Splash* (p.31) to generate spontaneous descriptions of people, landscapes, creatures, moods, etc.

- Combine *Dice Journey* with *Map Maker* (p.80), so that groups have a much clearer idea of where the narrative action takes place.

Countdown To A Story

This checklist, and the following activity – *Story Flowchart* (pp.183-5) – offer a structure within which the three main phases of the writing process – planning, writing, looking back – can take place. Here, and in the flowchart, *Imagine That...* activities can be used both to generate, link and refine ideas prior to presentation.

You may wish to adapt *Countdown To A Story* and *Story Flowchart* to suit the different ages and abilities of your students.

Basic activity

Before beginning to plan a story, have students consider the following:

21. Do I know what themes I am going to incorporate?

20. Do I want to write a particular type of story (see genre lists, pages 158-159)? What are my reasons for this?

19. What do I hope to achieve with this story, a) for myself, b) for the readers?

18. Has the basic idea been done before? By whom? How? With what result?

17. Am I bringing a fresh approach to the idea? What? How?

16. Am I using motifs deliberately, constructively, powerfully, originally?

15. Do I know enough about my characters?

14. Is the storyline mapped out clearly?

13. Do I have variations on the storyline, which I might prefer to use in the end?

12. Do I have an idea of how long the story will be?

11. Do I have a structure in terms of chapters and scenes?

10. Are the length and structure appropriate to the idea?

9. What is the background for the story? Is it appropriate?

8. Do I have the details of the time-and-place of the story clear in my mind?

7. Whose point of view will I take in the story? Why?

6. Have I considered other points of view (i.e. writing the story from the viewpoint of other characters)?

5. Do I feel confident that I can write this story?

4. Do I have a good first sentence/ paragraph/ scene?

3. Is there a better way of approaching the story than by starting at the beginning?

2. Do I have a final scene/ paragraph/ sentence in mind?

1. Am I ready to begin?

WRITE THE STORY

Now ask students to consider the following:

1. Am I broadly happy with the outcome?

2. Am I especially satisfied with particular passages or sentences in the story?

3.   Have I looked at them to find out why?

4. Am I especially unhappy with particular pieces of writing?

5. Have I looked at them to find out why?

6. Can I use anything in the story for future projects?

7. Can I repackage the story in other way – i.e. can I take this idea and turn it into a poem, a longer story, a story of a different genre, a play, etc.?

8. What have I learned about writing generally from this story?

9. What have I learned about characters, plots, backgrounds, genre from this story?

10. Is the presentation up to my best standard?

11. What is my next story?

12. Can I identify the themes within which I'm working...?

Ladder To The Moon

Ladder To The Moon illustrates a hierarchy of story-making which has probably existed as long as the human love of stories themselves. It may be helpful to refer to this list, along with the genre list on p.159, when you are doing activities in this section.

THE EARTH

Jokes

Shaggy Dog Stories

Personal Anecdotes

Family Stories

Ancestor Stories

Animal Stories

Cumulative Tales

Folk Stories

Horror and Ghost Stories

Fables

Legends and Historical Stories

Wonder Tales

Epic Tales

Sacred Stories

Creation and Origin Myths

THE MOON

Story Flowchart

This aid to creative writing started life as a way of helping writers' groups and participants on my writing courses. *Story Flowchart* (overleaf) is not a blueprint to be followed slavishly, but helps students to become sensitive to the components of creative writing, and aware of their own strengths, weaknesses, and direction. Where possible, reference has been made to activities in this book, but the truly creative 'Flowchart Explorer' is bound to find lots of other avenues of investigation.

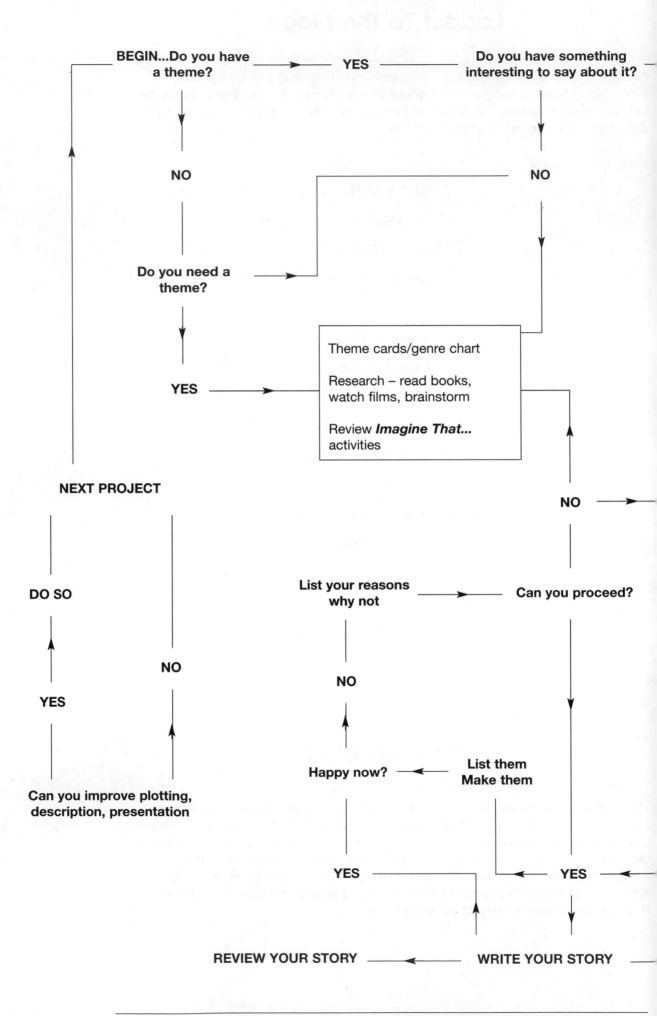

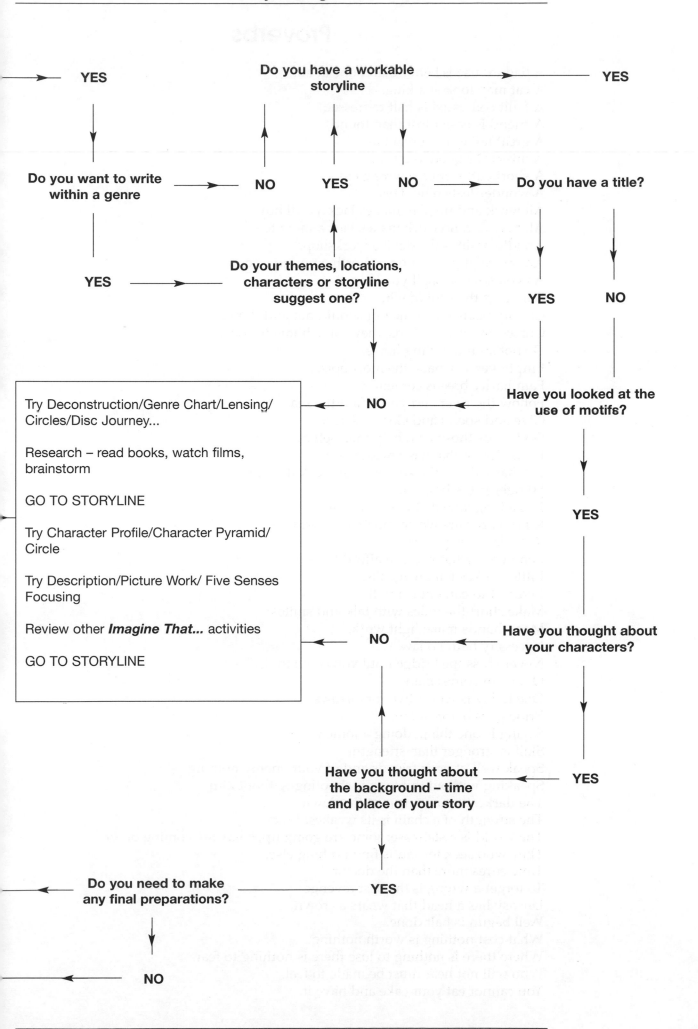

YES

Do you have a workable storyline

YES

Do you want to write within a genre

NO

YES

NO

Do you have a title?

YES

Do your themes, locations, characters or storyline suggest one?

YES

NO

NO

Have you looked at the use of motifs?

Try Deconstruction/Genre Chart/Lensing/ Circles/Disc Journey...

Research – read books, watch films, brainstorm

GO TO STORYLINE

Try Character Profile/Character Pyramid/ Circle

Try Description/Picture Work/ Five Senses Focusing

Review other *Imagine That...* activities

GO TO STORYLINE

YES

NO

Have you thought about your characters?

NO

Have you thought about the background – time and place of your story

YES

YES

Do you need to make any final preparations?

YES

NO

Proverbs

A bad excuse is better than none at all.
A cat may look at a king.
A fault confessed is half redressed.
A friend is easier lost than found.
A great talker is a great liar.
A miss is as good as a mile.
A short cut is often a wrong cut.
A wonder lasts nine days.
All work and no play makes Jack a dull boy.
All play and no work makes Jack a mere toy.
An idle brain is the devil's workshop.
An ounce of prevention is worth a pound of cure.
As you sow, so shall you reap.
Brevity is the soul of wit.
Charity begins at home but should not end there.
Curses are like chickens, they come home to roost.
Do not spur a willing horse.
Empty vessels make the most noise.
Familiarity breeds contempt.
Follow the river and you'll find the sea.
Give and spend and God will send.
God helps those who help themselves.
He is richest that has fewest wants.
He that will eat the kernel must crack the nut.
Hunger is the best sauce.
It is a long lane that has no turning.
Kind words are worth much and cost little.
Knowledge is power.
Lend only what you can afford to lose.
Little strokes fell great oaks.
Live not to eat, but eat to live.
Make short the miles with talk and smiles.
Many hands make light work.
Necessity hath no law.
Never cross the bridge until you come to it.
Of one ill comes many.
One today is worth two tomorrows.
Pride goes before a fall.
Saying is one thing, doing another.
Skill is stronger than strength.
Speak well of your friends and of your enemy nothing.
Speaking without thinking is shooting without aim.
The darkest hour is nearest the dawn.
The strength of a chain is its weakest link.
The world is a staircase; some are going up, some are coming down.
They who seek for faults find nothing else.
Time cures more than the doctor.
To forget a wrong is the best revenge.
Uneasy lies a head that wears a crown.
Well begun is half done.
What cost nothing is worth nothing.
Where there is nothing to lose there is nothing to fear.
Who will not hear must be made to feel.
You cannot eat your cake and have it.

Explorer – Training Activities For Teachers

As you will have gathered, my opinion is that what I call the Ping Process – that wonderful moment when an idea pops into your conscious mind – happens because of an attitude towards creative thinking, as much as it does because of games and activities that stimulate it. I also feel that the best way to teach the process, whether it be the techniques of creativity *per se*, or as they might be applied to a body of knowledge, is to generate and play with ideas oneself. As teachers we ought to practise what we preach.

Thus, there follows a kind of 'training ground' to strengthen the creative muscles, which I hope you'll attempt and enjoy. But before you begin, write down six ideas that you feel might help you to get the most out of the exercise: these can relate to good working practice, attitude, taking ideas further, and so on. Compare your list with the *Ping Process* on page 8.

The exercises employ most of the basic skills and techniques described in this book. For a reminder about the principles involved, and for more guidance, turn to the pages indicated. Skim through the exercises, attempting the ones that appeal to you most. Afterwards you might reflect on why any of them didn't appeal to you. When you've had enough, see if you can define a helpful attitude towards creative learning, and any principles you feel would be effective in promoting it.

Exercise 1.   Decision Dice (see p.15)

Devise six ways of using decision dice as part of day-to-day classroom activities (see *Dice Journey*, p.177 for a reminder of how to use the dice). One way of approaching this exercise is to think of broad headings as guides – emotions, geographical features, dates, natural phenomena, actions, creatures etc.

For example: Emotions/Actions

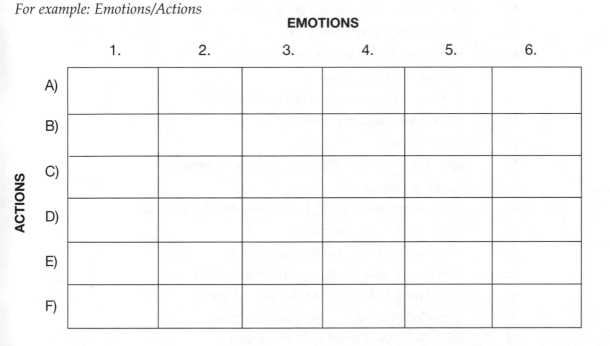

	EMOTIONS					
	1.	2.	3.	4.	5.	6.
A)						
B)						
C)						
D)						
E)						
F)						

ACTIONS

Exercise 2. Symbols (see p.45)

a) Devise an explanation for the symbol below.

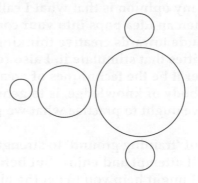

b) Now design ten new symbols and explain the significance of each.

Exercise 3. Story Tree (see p.168)

Below is a story tree skeleton and a list of statements. Pick a statement by using the first letter of your surname: if your surname begins with A, then use statement A as the initial premise on which your plotting will be based. Jot down your ideas for developing the plot(s). You are simply exploring narratives in this exercise, so the briefest notes only will be required for the ends of the branches.

A - consider your needs and the environment.

B - partnerships are likely.

C - be sensitive to signals and coincidence.

D - it's time for a parting or separation.

E - be strong and determined now.

F - you are about to break into new areas.

G - things happen to limit you.

H - you move into a fertile environment.

I - look to your defences.

J - to protect now will prevent trouble later.

K - possessions become more important.

L - joy is coming to you soon.

M - soon you will reap the harvest of your efforts.

N - openings lie ahead.

O - if you want something, be prepared to fight for it.

P - this is a time of new growth.

Q - move on and see obstacles removed.

R - don't fight, just go along with circumstances.

S - everything is about to suffer disturbance.

T - important messages are about to arrive.

U - be patient, you stand on a threshold.

V - a difficult problem is solved.

W - events stand still, so be patient.

Y - the whole thing; look at it again.

Z - the unknown – wait and see.

STORY TREE

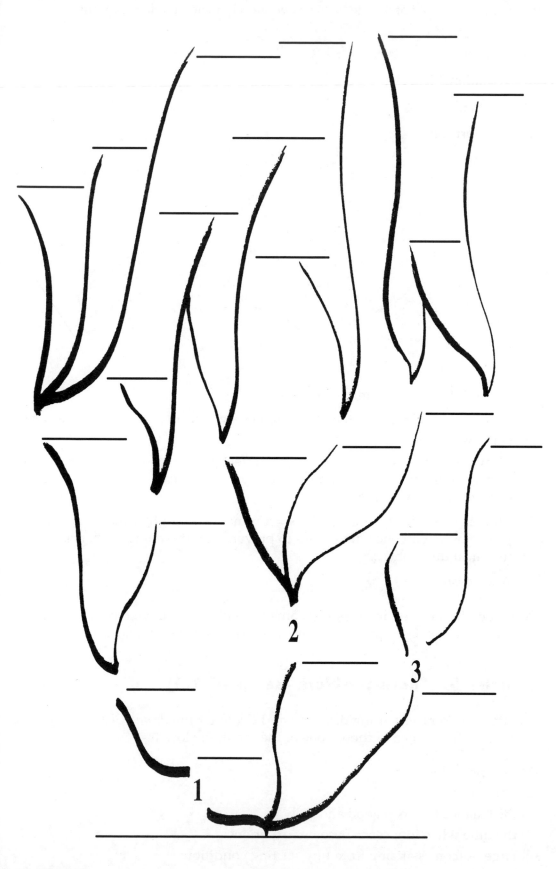

Initial Premise: _____

Exercise 4. Overlapping Circles (see p.47)

Imagine that the circles below represent people, or themes, events, genres, or a mixture of these or other ideas. First decide what each circle represents:

1) Travel

2) Relationships

3) Difficulty

4) Opportunity

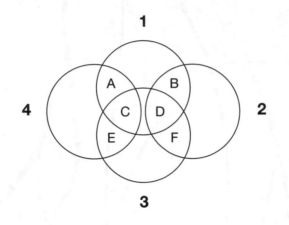

In this case, the overlaps might be:

A - travel + opportunity = the chance to get away from it all / a year out / an expedition...

B - travel + relationships = how this will affect people close to you / people you meet on the journey / how the journey transforms your relationships and attitude towards them...

C - travel + difficulty + relationships = a romantic encounter that leads to problems / someone who wishes to prevent you travelling / financial or technical difficulties...

And so on ...

Now look in the overlap areas and come up with ideas of what could be happening there. Use appropriate *Imagine That...* devices to help you.

Exercise 5. Character Work (see p.117-119)

Create two characters using dice rolls and *Character Profile and Character Pyramid* templates. Roll a dice to choose one of the themes below...

1) unexpected power

2) transformation

3) the balance between good and evil

4) the time when innocence becomes experience

5) large outcomes arising from tiny starting conditions

6) daring to defy

Now roll a twelve-sided dice to choose an emotional basis for your two characters, from the selection below...

1) terror
2) fury
3) jealousy
4) regret
5) anticipation
6) embarrassment
7) pride
8) excitement
9) nostalgia
10) exhilaration
11) love
12) awe

Character A: _____ Character B: _____

Roll the dice on a 1-6 scale to see when you'll 'step into the story' (1 = beginning; 6 = end)... Now use the dialogue sheet template below to write an exchange between your two principal characters at that point in the narrative, based on the theme and emotions you've rolled.

1) _____ ___ _____ – _____, _____ .

2) " _____! _____ ___ __ _____ _____ ."

3) " _____ _____ __ _____ ___. _____ ____?"

4) " ____ ____ _____ _____, _____..."

5) " _____`_, _____ _____."

6) " _____?"

7) " ____ _____ ___: ____ _____ _____.....?"

8) " _____ – _____!"

9) " `_____ _____ ____ __ __.` _____ ___ __."

10) " _____ ___!"

Exercise 6. Odd One Out (see p.30)

Devise reasons why each item in the following lists could be the odd-one-out.

a) bramble   orange   banana   lemon   walnut
b) canary   eagle   pigeon   magpie   robin
c) hawthorn   palm   beech   chestnut oak
d) tomato   journey   excursion voyage   trip
e) chair   carpet   wardrobe   stool   table

Exercise 7. Mythology (see p.161)

Conceive brief mythological narratives to explain the following phenomena...

a) Why does water freeze?
b) Why did cats allow themselves to be domesticated?
c) Why do shooting stars fall to Earth?
d) Why did the red squirrel become grey?
e) Why does the bumblebee fly?

Exercise 8. Invent-A-Word (see p.37)

Create definitions for the following word (including part-of-speech and etymology).

a) Zyme
b) Untrank
c) Reib
d) Mittly
e) Corvel

Exercise 9. Board Game (see p.97)

Devise a theme and rules of a board game based on the template below...

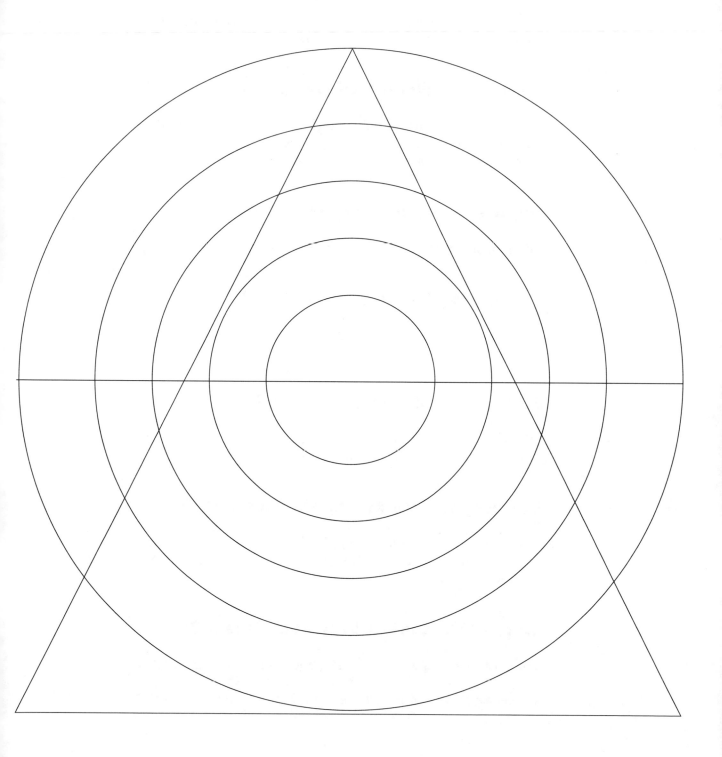

Exercise 10. How To Prevent (see p.95).

Think of ten ways of preventing cats from wailing in the night.

Exercise 11. Proverbs (see p.175)

Look back at the themes listed in the *Character Work* (pp.190-191) exercise and use each of them to create a new proverb.

Exercise 12. World Map (see p.84)

Shade-in a world map blank according to your personal prejudices. (If this is too threatening, shade in the map according to what you feel is your degree of knowledge about the world – or choose a theme of your own.)

Exercise 13. Alpha Team (see p.107)

Think of six exciting missions for the Alpha Team.

Exercise 14. Theme Card (see p.17)

Create a theme card, either using the themes above (see Character Work), or one of your own choice.

Exercise 15. Map Maker (see p.80)

Flip open an atlas at random and stick a pin in the page. Visualise what that location might look like and write a brief description.

Exercise 16. Free Association (see p.21)

Choose a word at random from this book. Close your eyes or gaze at a blank space, and see where your thoughts take you for a few minutes. Note down any interesting ideas...

Exercise 17. Context Sentences (see p.90)

Think of twenty questions to ask about the following sentence:

As soon as she walked into the room, she knew the calm before the storm was now over.

Exercise 18. Themed Acrostic (see p.35)

Come up with six items for each letter of the word below, each pertinent to the theme...

G

A

M

E

S

T

E

R

Exercise 19. Parallel World (see p.92)

Think of six headings on which you can hang ideas about the consequences of living in the parallel world below, then scribble ideas down as they come to you:

In this world, there are two distinct races, the human Day People, and the almost-human Night People.

Exercise 20. Minisagas (see p.173)

Write a micro-, mini-, midi-, maxi-, or mega-saga (or one of your own devising) based on the parallel world above.

Exercise 21. Control Panel (see p.170)

Use the template on page 171, or devise a different one of your own. Use a dice on three of the controls, 1-3 = turn down, 4-6 = turn up. Now apply those controls to the story of Cinderella (or one of your choice), and jot down interesting ideas and variations.

Exercise 22. Freeze-frame (see p.71)

Carry out the freeze-frame technique on the paragraph below.

She woke to see Mark's worried face in front of her. It rippled, as though she was seeing it through water. She tried to smile, to show him she was all right – that she had survived. But somehow her body seemed distant and strange, and she wasn't sure if the smile had worked properly at all.

Panic Station Bowkett. S (FunFax Horror, Henderson Publications, 1996)

Exercise 25. Three Mexicans Weeing In A Well (see p.40)

Think of six things the shape below could represent.

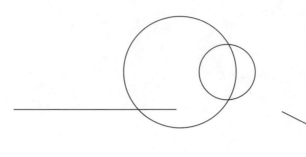

Exercise 26. Symbols (see p.45)

Devise a explanation for the symbol below.

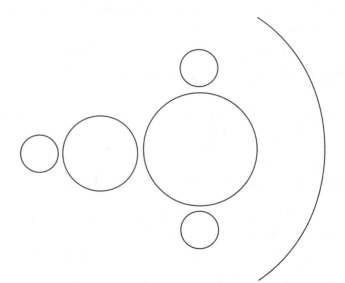

BIBLIOGRAPHY:

All of these books have been helpful to me in one way or another in the writing of *Imagine That...*, and in the evolution of the games and workshops it contains. Where one of my techniques has been based on an idea or activity from elsewhere, then I have endeavoured to credit the originator and acknowledge my debt of gratitude. Many of the references will be useful to the *Explorer* section (p.187) in providing material for workshops and projects, while others give valuable insights into the creative process and how the techniques I've offered can be best exploited, developed and improved.

Ash, R., **Incredible Comparisons** (Dorling Kindersley, 1996)

Asimov, I., **Words Of Science** (Harrap, 1974)

Augarde, T., **The Oxford Guide To Word Games** (O.U.P., 1983)

Barnes, D., Britton, J., Rosen, H., **Language, The Learner And The School** (Penguin, 1971)

Beare. G, **Heath Robinson Machines and Inventions** (C Beetles, 1997)

Bentine, M. **Open Your Mind: the quest for creative thinking** (Bantam, 1990)

Betteridge, D., Buckby, M., Wright, A., **Games For Language Learning** (O.U.P., 1981)

Bowkett, S., **Meditations For Busy People** (Thorsons, 1996)

For The Moon There Is The Cloud: tales in the Zen tradition (Collins Pathways Reading Scheme, Collins Educational, 1996)

Brandes, D., and Phillips, H., (**Gamesters Handbook** Hutchinson 1979).

Briggs, K., **British Folklore And Legends: a sampler** (Granada, 1978)

Brookes, R., Latham, J., Rex, H., **Developing Oral Skills** (Heinemann, 1986)

Brown, R., & Lawrence, M., **Mammals: Tracks & Signs** (Macdonald, 1983)

Brownjohn, A. & S., **Meet And Write: a teaching anthology of contemporary poetry** (Hodder & Stoughton, 1985)

Bruya, B. (trans), **Zen Speaks by Tsai Chih Chung** (Aquarian, 1994)

Button, J., **A Dictionary Of Green Ideas** (Routledge, 1988)

Buzan, T., **Use Your Head** (BBC Books, 1993)

Capra, F., **The Turning Point** (Flamingo, 1984)

Chetwynd, T., **A Dictionary For Dreamers** (Thorsons, 1993)

A Dictionary Of Symbols (Thorsons, 1993)

Clarke, A. C., **Profiles Of The Future** (Pan, 1964)

Clute, J., **Science Fiction: the illustrated encyclopedia** (Dorling Kindersley, 1995)

De Bono, E., **Lateral Thinking** (Pelican, 1984)

De Bono, E., **Teach Your Child How To Think** (Pelican, 1993)

DfEE, **The National Curriculum** (H.M.S.O., 1995)

Dewhurst-Maddock, O., **The Book Of Sound Therapy** (Gaia, 1993)

Dixon, D., **After Man: a zoology of the future** (BCA, 1981)

The New Dinosaurs: an alternative evolution (Grafton, 1988)

Man After Man: an anthropology of the future (Blandford, 1990)

Dorling Kindersley Ultimate Visual Dictionary (Dorling Kindersley, 1997)

Douglas, T., **The Complete Guide To Advertising** (Macmillan, 1985)

Duff, A., and Maley, A. , **Drama Techniques In Language Learning**
(C.U.P., 1980)

Edwards, B., **Drawing On The Artist Within: how to release your hidden**
creativity (Collins, 1987)

Ekwall, E., **The Concise Oxford Dictionary Of English Place-Names**
(O.U.P., 1981).

Elliott-Kemp, H., **Developing Poetic Writing In The Middle Years** (PAVIC
Publications, Sheffield City Polytechnic, 1982)

Elliott-Kemp, H., **Fostering Creativity** (PAVIC, 1984)

Ferguson, M., **The Aquarian Conspiracy** (Paladin, 1986)

Gardner, W. H. (Ed), **Gerard Manley Hopkins: Poetry & Prose** (Penguin, 1970)

Gawain, S., Creative Visualisation (Bantam Books, 1982)

Gilioli, P., **Mindscapes: psychological mazes for personality insight** (Collier
Books, 1984)

Goldberg, P., **The Intuitive Edge** (Turnstone Press, 1985)

Good, M., **Write On** (ALBSCU / Channel 4 / Yorkshire TV, 1986)

Goleman, D. **Emotional Intelligence** (Bloomsbury Paperbacks, 1996)

Graves, R., **The Greek Myths** (Penguin, 1955)

Green Party Working Group, **Routes To Change** (a collection of essays for
Green Education, 1988.)

Gregory, R. L., **Eye And Brain** (World University Library, 1972)

Greig, S., Pike, G., Selby, D., **Greenprints For Changing Schools** (WWF /
Kogan Page, 1989)

Grigson, G., **The Shell Country Alphabet** (Michael Joseph, 1966)

Hall, C. & E., Leech, A., **Scripted Fantasy In The Classroom** (Routledge, 1990)

Halliwell, J.O., **Popular Rhymes And Nursery Tales Of England** (Bodley
Head, 1970)

Hewitt, J., **Teach Yourself Relaxation** (Hodder & Stoughton, 1985)

Hittleman, R., **Guide To Yoga Meditation** (Bantam, 1969)

Instone, I., **The Teaching Of Problem Solving** (Longman, 1988)

Joicey, H. B., **An Eye On The Environment: an art education project** (Bell &
Hyman / WWF, 1986)

Kohler, M., **The Secrets Of Relaxation** (Pan, 1973)

Lewis, D., **Mind Skills** (Souvenir Press, 1987)

Lewis R., **The Schools Guide To Open Learning** (National Extension
College, 1986)

Markham, U., **Visualisation** (Element, 1991)

Masterman, L., **Teaching About Television** (Macmillan, 1983)
Television Mythologies (Camedia / Routledge, 1988)

Michell, J., **Simulacra** (Thames & Hudson, 1979)

Morley, D., **Under The Rainbow: writers and artists in schools**
(Bloodaxe, 1991)

Morris, D., **Bodywatching** (Jonathan Cape, 1985)

Murphy, J., **The Power Of Your Subconscious Mind** (Simon and Schuster, 1991)

Nicholls, P. (Ed.), **The Science Of Science Fiction** (Michael Joseph, 1982)

Nilsson, L., **Close To Nature** (Pantheon Books, 1984)

Opie, I. & P., **The Lore And Language Of SchoolChildren** (O.U.P., 1959)
Childrens' Games In Street And Playground (O.U.P., 1969)
The Classic Fairy Tales (O.U.P., 1975)

O'Rourke, R. and Robinson, M., **Running Good Writing Groups: a resource pack** (University of Leeds, 1996)

Ostrander, S., Schroeder, L., **Cosmic Memory: the supermemory revolution** (Simon and Schuster, 1993)

Page, M., **Visualisation** (Aquarian, 1990)

Pease, A., **Body Language** (Sheldon Press, 1987)

Pike, G. and Selby, D., **Global Teacher, Global Learner** (Hodder & Stoughton, 1988)

Postman, N. and Weingartner, C., **Teaching As A Subversive Activity** (Penguin, 1972)

Purkis, C. and Guerin, C., **English Language Games** (Macmillan, 1984)

Scott-Macnab, J. (Ed. British Edition), **Reader`s Digest Marvels And Mysteries Of The Human Mind,** 1992)

Ronan, C. (Gen. Ed.), **Science Explained** (Doubleday, 1993)

Sagan, C., **Murmurs Of Earth: the Voyager Interstellar Record** (Hodder and Stoughton, 1979)

Shayer, D., **Ways With Words** (Evans, 1990)

Smith, A., **Accelerated Learning In The Classroom** (Network Educational Press, 1996)

Stock, G., **The Book Of Questions** (Thorsons, 1987)

Thouless, R. H., **Straight And Crooked Thinking** (Pan, 1953)

Toffler, A., **The Third Wave** (Pan, 1981)

Ueland, B., **If You Want To Write: releasing your creative spirit** (Element, 1994)

Van Oech, R., **A Whack On The Side Of The Head: how you can be more creative** (Thorsons, 1990)

Watts, A., **Tao: the watercourse way** (Pelican, 1981)

Wilson, C., **Frankenstein's Castle: the right brain, door to wisdom** (Ashgrove Press, 1988)

Woodlander, D., **How Our Language Grew** (Collins Educational, 1988)

INDEX

Imagine That… A Handbook of Creative Learning Activities for the Classroom

STEVE BOWKETT was a teacher of English for 18 years in a Leicestershire High School. He is now a full-time writer and also a qualified hypnotherapist.

He was born and brought up in the mining valleys of South Wales, and his childhood experiences have been an important influence in the development of his fiction. Steve began writing at the age of thirteen when, purely by chance, an irate French mistress sent him to the naughty corner and told him to 'get on with something'. He wrote his first unconstrained story about a girl he'd fallen for and an invading green blob monster. He has not looked back since.

Steve's early published work consisted of fantasy for teenagers. He has since diversified into adult and teen horror, teen romance, mainstream fiction for pre-teens, fiction for younger readers, non-fiction, and poetry for all ages.

In his spare time, Steve enjoys rock music, cooking oriental food, drinking beer and cleaning up after his two cats. "I am fond of cats," Steve maintains,"because they love me for myself and because I feed them promptly three times a day." He does not love venomous creatures, nor those that are larger than himself or have sharper teeth, quite as much.

When asked what advice he would give to an aspiring writer, Steve always replies:

> *Have faith in yourself.*
> *Be prepared to work hard.*
> *Ideas are like plants. Cultivate the seeds and the trees will grow.*

Publications

Spellbinder (teen fantasy) – Gollancz, 1985 / Pan, 1988

The Copy Cat Plan – Blackwell, 1986

Gameplayers (teen fantasy) – Gollancz, 1986 / Pan, 1988

***Dualists** (teen fantasy) – Gollancz, 1987 / Pan, 1989

Catch & Other Stories (genre) – Gollancz, 1988 / Pan, 1990

Frontiersville High (teen SF) – Gollancz, 1990

The Community (adult horror) – Pan, 1993

The Bidden (adult horror) – Pan, 1994

A Rare Breed (adult horror) – Pan, 1996

Panic Station (teen horror) – Henderson, 1996

Dinosaur Day (young fantasy) – Heinemann, 1996

For The Moon There Is The Cloud (tales in the Zen tradition) – Collins, Pathways reading scheme, 1996.

The World's Smallest Werewolf – Macdonald, Shivery Storybooks, 1996.

Meditations For Busy People (How To Stop Worrying & Stay Calm) – HarperCollins, 1996 (USA 1997).

The Web 2 – Dreamcastle (teen SF) – Orion Children's Books, 1997.

Prior to the publication of his first novel, Steve's short stories and poetry were broadcast on BBC Radio Leicester, BRMB (Birmingham) and Radio Northampton, and published in a large number of small press magazines. More recently, he has had short stories published in *Interzone,* and the small press magazines *Peeping Tom, Kimota* and the British Fantasy Society publication *Chills.*

To date, Steve has written over fifty novels, several hundred short stories, over five hundred poems, several plays and works of non-fiction.

* Film rights for *Dualists* optioned by Walt Disney 1991-93.

Other Titles from Network Educational Press

THE SCHOOL EFFECTIVENESS SERIES

Book 1: *Accelerated Learning in the Classroom* by Alistair Smith

Book 2: *Effective Learning Activities* by Chris Dickinson

Book 3: *Effective Heads of Department* by Phil Jones & Nick Sparks

Book 4: *Lessons are for Learning* by Mike Hughes

Book 5: *Effective Learning in Science* by Paul Denley and Keith Bishop

Book 6: *Raising Boys' Achievement* by Jon Pickering

Book 7: *Effective Provision for Able & Talented Children* by Barry Teare

Book 8: *Effective Careers Education & Guidance* by Andrew Edwards and Anthony Barnes

Book 9: *Best behaviour and Best behaviour FIRST AID* by Peter Relf, Rod Hirst, Jan Richardson and Georgina Youdell

Best behaviour FIRST AID
(pack of 5 booklets)

Book 10: *The Effective School Governor* by David Marriott
(including free audio tape)

Book 11: *Improving Personal Effectiveness for Managers in Schools* by James Johnson

Book 12: *Making Pupil Data Powerful* by Maggie Pringle and Tony Cobb

Book 13: *Closing the Learning Gap* by Mike Hughes

Book 14: *Getting Started* by Henry Leibling

Book 15: *Leading the Learning School* by Colin Weatherley

Book 16: *Adventures in Learning* by Mike Tilling

Book 17: *Strategies for Closing the Learning Gap* by Mike Hughes

Book 18: *Classroom Management* by Philip Waterhouse and Chris Dickinson

ACCELERATED LEARNING SERIES
General Editor: **Alistair Smith**

Accelerated Learning in Practice by Alistair Smith

The ALPS Approach: Accelerated Learning in Primary Schools
by Alistair Smith and Nicola Call

MapWise by Oliver Caviglioli and Ian Harris

The ALPS Resource Book by Alistair Smith and Nicola Call

EDUCATION PERSONNEL MANAGEMENT SERIES

These new Education Personnel Management handbooks will help headteachers, senior managers and governors to manage a broad range of personnel issues.

The Well Teacher – management strategies for beating stress, promoting staff health and reducing absence
by Maureen Cooper

Managing Challenging People – dealing with staff conduct
by Bev Curtis and Maureen Cooper

Managing Poor Performance – handling staff capability issues
by Bev Curtis and Maureen Cooper

Managing Allegations Against Staff – personnel and child protection issues in schools
by Maureen Cooper

Managing Recruitment and Selection – appointing the best staff
by Bev Curtis and Maureen Cooper

Managing Redundancies – dealing with reduction and reorganisation of staff
by Bev Curtis and Maureen Cooper

VISIONS OF EDUCATION SERIES

The Unfinished Revolution by John Abbott and Terry Ryan

The Child is Father of the Man by John Abbott

The Learning Revolution by Jeanette Vos and Gordon Dryden

Wise-Up by Guy Claxton

THE LITERACY COLLECTION

Helping With Reading by Anne Butterworth and Angela White

Class Talk by Rosemary Sage

OTHER TITLES FROM NEP

Effective Resources for Able and Talented Children by Barry Teare

More Effective Resources for Able and Talented Children by Barry Teare

Self-Intelligence by Stephen Bowkett
